Mediterranean Wines of Place

Mediterranean Wines of Place

A Celebration of Heritage Grapes

AL LEONARD

LOCKWOOD PRESS

Mediterranean Wines of Place: A Celebration of Heritage Grapes

ISBN

978-1-948488-43-3 (paperback)

978-1-948488-44-0 (PDF eBook)

Cover design by Susanne Wilhelm

Library of Congress Cataloguing-in-Publication Data

Names: Leonard, Al, author.
Title: Mediterranean wines of place : a celebration of heritage grapes / Al Leonard.
Description: Atlanta : Lockwood Press, [2020] | Summary: "In Mediterranean Wines of Place, Al Leonard, a professor of classical archaeology and wine aficionado, pairs his love of the Mediterranean world with wines that are crafted from the heritage grapes that have been so much a part of its history"– Provided by publisher.
Identifiers: LCCN 2020013649 (print) | LCCN 2020013650 (ebook) | ISBN 9781948488433 (paperback) | ISBN 9781948488440 (adobe pdf)
Subjects: LCSH: Wine and wine making–Mediterranean Region–History. | Mediterranean Region–Description and travel. | Mediterranean Region–History.
Classification: LCC TP559.M47 L46 2020 (print) | LCC TP559.M47 (ebook) | DDC 641.2/2094–dc23
LC record available at https://lccn.loc.gov/2020013649

LC ebook record available at https://lccn.loc.gov/2020013650

Printed in the United States on acid-free paper.

To Siduri

Beside the sea Siduri lives,
The woman of the vine,
The maker of the wine.
She sits in her garden at the edge of the sea,
With the golden vats that the gods have given her.

The Epic of Gilgamesh, Tablet X (adapted), 2000–1200 BCE

Table of Contents

Random Thoughts, with Glass in Hand – An Introduction

The Dionysus Cup, one of the best known works of ancient Greek vase painting, by the Attic Black-figure potter Exekias, 540–530 BCE.

Original: Staatliche Antikensammlungen, München, Inv. no. 2044. Drawing adaptation © Susanne Wilhelm.

What turns a beer drinking, dirt-archaeologist into a wine aficionado? Well, in my case, it was the love of a wonderful woman: my late wife of twenty-plus years, Mary Halsell Banks. It was she who first introduced me to the wines of California's Santa Barbara County and later to the vineyards of Sonoma's Russian River Appellation.

Although it was Mary who opened my door to the world of wine, it was Karen MacNeil who pushed me through. In the late 1990's, as an instructor at the newly-opened Culinary Institute of America at Greystone in St. Helena (Napa Valley, CA) and while writing *The Wine Bible,*[1] Karen offered an introductory class on wine. I enrolled, and on the very first day I knew that I was hooked! Not simply hooked by the complexity of wine as a beverage but, equally as important for me, the degree to which each wine was a reflection of the place where it was produced. Certainly, wine has a geophysical *terroir* such as weather, temperatures, and soil, but it also has a strong historical *terroir* that paradoxically lies deeper in the dirt—where archaeologists are more at home. I went on to enjoy several other, excellent wine courses at the CIA's Rudd Center for Professional Wine Studies, partially supported by a Robert A. Parker Wine Advocate Fellowship. During this time I also discovered the Society of Wine Educators which I joined in 1999 and of which I have been a member ever since.

Throughout my academic career, I have been what is known archaeologically as a "pottery guy." On a dig I will spend hours sifting through piles of broken pottery, trying to hear the story that every fragment has to tell and how, taken as a group, that story could be expanded to reveal information about the people who had once possessed them. Potsherds can tell us a lot—if we will listen. Different clays are chosen for different types of pots. Different shapes can indicate specific functions. Is this sherd from an open form, i.e., a plate or piece of dinner ware, or is it from a closed form such as a jar meant to store or transport a liquid or a solid? What might that commodity have been? Was it a local product or was it

[1] *The Wine Bible* was first published in 2001 by Workman Press and the completely revised and up-dated second edition (1000+ pages) was produced in 2015, also by Workman Press. Karen is the creator and presently Chairman Emeritus of The Rudd Center for Professional Wine Studies at the Culinary Institute of America at Greystone.

something traded from afar? And, more recently, what scientific tests are available to coax more of the story from these small, inanimate pieces of *terra cotta*?

An excellent example of the fruits that such a conversation offers can be found at the archaeological site of Godin Tepe, located far from the Mediterranean, deep in the Zagros mountains of Iran. It was late in the 1960s, at a time when our earliest physical—as opposed to literary—evidence for the first appearance of wine dated sometime in the early First Millennium BCE. But then at Godin Tepe, in a building dated between 3500 and 3000 years BCE, T. Cuyler Young and his colleagues from the Royal Ontario Museum in Toronto excavated a deposit of pottery. One of these pots, a large jar, bore an unusually narrow neck, making it a perfect container for the transport or storage of a liquid. But surprisingly, and more importantly, the interior surface of that jar still retained residual traces of its original contents.

At this point, modern science again stepped in. Chemical analysis of a sample of this residue by Patrick McGovern and Rudolph Michel of the University of Pennsylvania identified the presence of tartaric acid. This indicated that the jar had once contained a fermented grape product and thus, by extension, that the pot had originally contained wine. Such an unexpected result, from an archaeological deposit that had been shown by ^{14}C analysis to date to the second half of the Fourth Millennium BCE proved *scientifically* that human knowledge of wine production was over 5,000 years old!

The implications of the Godin Tepe jar and its contents sparked renewed interest in the early history of wine. Bioanthropologist Solomon Katz and molecular archaeologist Patrick McGovern (both at the University of Pennsylvania) approached Robert Mondavi (and his family) who agreed to sponsor and host an international symposium on *The Origin and Ancient History of Wine* to be held at the Mondavi Winery in Napa Valley (CA) in 1991. Also supporting the project was Jan Shrem, owner of Clos Pegase Winery. I was invited to be one of about two dozen participants and spoke on the early history of the transport vessel that eventually developed into the classic, two-handled amphora that has long been been associated with the maritime wine trade throughout the ancient Mediterranean World. The proceedings of the symposium were published in 1995.[2]

For over two decades I have been a speaker for various small ship programs in the Mediterranean including, *inter alia*, Archaeological Institute of America Tours as well as Smithsonian Journeys. I lecture predominantly on archaeology, art, food, and wine (both ancient and modern). When I discovered how interested many passengers were in the history of the local foods and traditional wines that we encountered, I began writing short pieces on culinary history. It is amazing how readily you are able to connect with a culture when you "break

2 *The Origins and Ancient History of Wine*, edited by Patrick E. McGovern, Stuart J. Fleming, and Solomon H. Katz (Gordon and Breach Publishers), 1995. The present author's contribution, "Canaanite Jars and the Late Bronze Age Ageo-Levantine Wine Trade," appears on pages 233–254.

bread" or "raise a glass" with the local populace. Eventually, I discovered my *alter ego*: The Time Traveling Gourmet ("He who puts history on your plate... and in your glass"). These short pieces were the genesis of the present book.

It is often said that to be a successful writer one must have an excellent editor. My *editrix* has been Mary Lannin whom my wife and I first met in 1998 at an all-day session on olive oil at CIA-Greystone. She was active in the wine industry (Winery Associates of Sonoma County and one of the founding partners of Murphy Goode Wines) and fascinated by archaeology. I was an archaeologist fascinated by wine. It was a perfect balance. Over the years Mary has read each of these fourteen chapters in their various stages, always offering sage advice and maintaining that much needed balance. Surprisingly, but fortunately, we have remained friends through it all.

Once edited, I would send each manuscript along with an assortment of related images to my friend Oscar Anderson whom I had first met almost fifty years ago when I was a graduate student at the University of Chicago's Oriental Institute. Although as a student Oscar had concentrated on ancient Mesopotamian languages, he went on to have a distinguished career in the field of design and publishing. Oscar would apply his magic to each of the manuscripts and transform my scribblings into a very attractive product. These I would mail to the people with whom I had traveled.

Over time, many of these readers suggested that I produce a small, portable booklet that would introduce travelers to wines made from some of the lesser-known grapes that are indigenous to the Mediterranean World. Oscar was in the design stage of such a volume when he called one Sunday afternoon. He said (without explanation) that he was in the hospital but that he had been thinking about the cover design and would be sending along some ideas early the next week. He never did, as he passed away a few days later. I owe a tremendous debt of gratitude to his wife, Jo Anderson, for locating and securing the relevant files. With the help of Walter Novak of Wabash College, Jo was able to get them forwarded to Susanne Wilhelm and Ian Stevens of ISD who had helped me with a previous book and, together with Billie Jean Collins of Lockwood Press, they brought this book to completion.

Over the years many others have contributed their time and/or their knowledge to this project. Some have shared their insight into a particular facet of wine or its history. Others have called my attention to specific grapes, sent me clippings, facilitated photographs, or simply listened patiently to my ramblings. I thank them all. And, at the expense of missing some, I list several of them on the next page, alphabetically by surname. Professional titles are omitted and affiliations may have changed.

Finally, this book is just the latest manifestation of the support and encouragement that I have received over the years from my family, especially from my sister Susan. To all I am truly grateful.

Thank you

George Athanas (Greek Wine Bureau – North America, EDOAO), Sofia Athanassopoulou (Fine Wines, Athens, Greece), Marian W. Baldy (California State University, Chico CA), Gloria Baxevanis (Smithsonian Journeys, Washington DC), Jan Birnbaum (Catahula, Callistoga CA), Bill & Jane Biers (University of Missouri-Columbia), Yiannis Boutaris (Boutari Wines, Naoussa, Greece), Bob Brousseau (Dallas, TX), Robin Brown (Watertown, MA), Jeremy Cassar (Marsovin Wines, Marsa, Malta), Linda & Tim Clougherty (Cloverdale, CA), Lauren Cummings (Archaeological Institute of America Tours, Walpole, NH), Suzana Davila (Café Poca Cosa, Tucson, AZ), William G. Dever (University of Arizona), Dana & Roger Dunn (St. Pete's Beach, FL), Gary Emmerich (Dry Creek Vineyard, Healdsburg, CA), Victor England (Classical Numismatic Group, LLC), Gioacchino Falsone (University of Palermo), Stuart J. Flemming (University of Pennsylvania), Tom & Cappie Garrett (Santa Rosa, CA), Andrea Gaylor & Rick Delope (Windsor, CA), Richard & Julia Geist (San Rafael, CA), Sandy Gerstung (Baltimore, MD), Randall Graham (Bonny Doon Vineyard, Bonny Doon, CA), Joseph Greene (Harvard University), Violet Grgich (Grgich Hills Estate, Rutherford, CA), Rick Hutchinson (Amphora Winery, Healdsburg, CA), Nancy Harmon Jenkins (CIA at Greystone, St. Helena, CA), David and Jeannie Hendin (New York, NY), Stavroula Korakou-Drakona (International Organization of Vine and Wine), Petros & Xenia Matekas (Villa Renos, Thera, Greece), Steve & Rebecca Lalonde (Healdsburg, CA), Barbara Lannin (Healdsburg, CA), Roxane Matsa (Domaine Matsa, Kantza, Attica, Greece), Alison McCarthy (Smithsonian Journeys), Georges Meekers (Founder, Wine Campus, Valletta, Malta), Marta González Miró (Marimar Estate Vineyards, Sebastopol, CA), Holly Peterson Mondavi (CIA at Greystone), Jim & Polly Muhly (Athens, Greece), Todd Nielsen (Archaeological Institute of America Tours, Walpole, NH), Yannis Paraskevopoulos (Gaia Wines, Nemea, Greece), René & Caryl Peron (Santa Rosa Junior College), Dave Ready (Murphy-Goode Winery and Winery Associates of Sonoma County, CA), Marlene Rice (Classical Numismatic Group, LLC), Taylan Sargin (Sensus Wine Boutique, Istanbul, Turkey), Jill Salayi (Workman Publishing, New York, NY), Danny Scordato (Vivace, Tucson AZ), Paul Sherman (ClipArt), Haroula Spinthiropoulou (New Wines of Greece, EDOAO, Athens, Greece), David Stare (Dry Creek Vineyard, Healdsburg, CA), Maritina Stavrakaki (Assistant Professor, The Agricultural University of Athens), Manolis N. Stavrakakis (Professor Emeritus, The Agricultural University of Athens), Joy Anne Sterling (Iron Horse Ranch and Winery, Sebastopol, CA), Lawrence & Terry Sterling (Iron Horse Ranch and Winery, Sebastopol, CA), Alan Tardi (Prosecco US Ambassador of Conegliano Valdobbiadene, Italy), Jonathan Tubb (The British Museum, London, Great Britain), Donna White (Vinkara Wines, Istanbul, Turkey), Janos Wilder (Downtown Kitchen + Cocktails, Tucson, AZ).

Athens

Greece

'he Parthenon (Temple of Athena Parthenos) sits majestically atop the Akropolis as a centuries-old eminder of the protection that the goddess has given to the city that bears her name.
hoto by Francesco Bandarin, © UNESCO (CC BY-SA 3.0 IGO).

Small fragments of chipped stone tools and tiny bits of prehistoric pottery bear witness to the passage of a myriad of nameless groups who were drawn to the Athenian Akropolis and the surrounding Plain of Attica by ivers and springs that have long since disappeared or been diverted. Richer inds from later tombs and structures demonstrate the city's slow but steady rowth throughout what archaeologists refer to as the Bronze and Iron Ages.

A silver Athenian coin of the 5th century BCE depicting Athena's owl, a sprig of olive, and the abbreviation "[of the] ATHE [nians]". Museum of Fine Arts, Lyon.
Photo by Marie-Lan Nguyen (Wikimedia Commons, CC BY 2.5).

t some point in the dim mist of this early history, the people of Attica developed special relationship with Athena. She was the beautiful and intelligent goddess vho was born fully armored from the brow of her divine father, Zeus. Her hold n her community was cemented when the city chose her gift, the olive, over ne spring offered to them by Poseidon. Both of these seminal events were elebrated in the sculpture that graced the Temple of Athena Parthenos (The 'arthenon) that had been built for her—and paid for with tax money—by the itizens of Athens. This was part of a program of beautification carried out on the kropolis during the reign of Perikles in the middle of the 5th century BCE.

Athena, patroness of Athens. In the 5th century BCE the sculptor Pheidias crafted a 40-foot chryselephantine (gold and ivory) image of her to serve as the cult statue in the Parthenon. The Glyptothek, Munich.
Photo by Marie-Lan Nguyen (Wikimedia Commons, CC BY 2.5).

To the north of the Akropolis stretched the ancient city's agora. Often translated simply as "marketplace", the agora was that and much more: council house, law courts, administrative offices, etc. It was here that Socrates and Aristotle walked and taught as well as a host of other philosophers and thinkers whose names have come down to us today: Stoics, Cynics, Epicureans, and the like. It was here that many of the mechanics of our modern democracies were invented, tried out, improved upon, and eventually passed on to the Romans whose emperors alternatively celebrated and neglected the city's institutions.

The highpoint for Roman Athens was undoubtedly the reign of Emperor Hadrian (117–138 CE) who graced the city with a magnificent building program that rivaled that of Perikles centuries earlier. It was Hadrian who completed the huge temple to Olympian Zeus, under construction for almost seven centuries, with over 100 columns more than 50 feet in height. The grateful Athenians, in return, rewarded him with the title Soter ("Savior"), further supporting the contention made by St. Paul a generation earlier that Athens was a city "wholly given to idolatry" (Acts XVII: 16).

After steadily shelling the Akropolis for five days in 1687, the Venetian forces of Francesco Morosini hit a Turkish powder magazine that blew the center out of the Parthenon, which was then being used as a mosque (note the minaret).
Photo: Francesco Fanelli, 1590-1653 (PD).

Over the next few centuries, Paul's new deity eclipsed Athena. When Constantine the Great bypassed Athens and chose Byzantium (renaming it Constantinople) as the capital of the Eastern Roman Empire, the writing for Athens was on the wall. The city kept its university but outward manifestations of the city's pagan past were increasingly less tolerated. Finally, in 529 CE, the death knell rang: Emperor Justinian commanded that all pagan temples—including the Parthenon—were to be closed or turned into churches. Slowly and quietly the City of Athena began to slip into obscurity until, shortly after Mehmet II conquered Constantinople in 1453, Athens passed almost unnoticed into the domain of the Ottoman Turk. So began centuries of struggle between the Crescent and the Cross, memories of which can still spark hostilities in parts of the Mediterranean World today.

The Turkish occupation of Athens lasted until the 1830s when, at the conclusion of the Greek War of Independence, the Great Powers of Europe dispatched Prince Othon (Otto), the teenage son of King Ludwig of Bavaria, to become the first king of the newly independent country. Once again Greece was on the mend, and the newly reinvigorated Athens began to blossom in her role as its capital city.

Despite Greek involvement in the Balkan Wars, Athens continued to flourish during La Belle Époque, but she saw her fortunes reversed by foreign occupation during World War II, a devastating Civil War, and years of rule by a military junta—all in quick succession. Resilient and always industrious, the citizens of present-day Athens have embarked on yet another program to beautify their city. Pedestrian walkways and green zones have transformed the slopes of the Akropolis and large areas of the city into archaeological parks, while, high above them, large cranes are hard at work slowly restoring Athena's temple to its former glory.

Local Grape Varietals

It is said that when Dionysos first arrived on Attic soil he was befriended by a man named Ikarios. In return, the god presented him with a vine cutting and taught him the art of making wine. While it is not recorded which grape varietal was bestowed on the lucky Ikarios, it may have been one of these indigenous or traditional grapes that are extremely well suited to the long, dry days of the Attic summer.

Savatiano (Sa-va-tya-NO) is a vigorous, high yielding white varietal that accounts for about 90% of the grape grown around Athens today. By itself, Savatiano can produce a dry, very food-friendly wine, with aromas of citrus blossoms and peach. Semeli Wines (named after Dionysos' mother by Zeus) offers two good examples (**Semeli White** and **Amaryllis White**) made from fruit grown on the higher elevations of Mt. Pendeli in northern Attica, as does Roxani Matsa whose **Domaine Matsa** (produced in cooperation with Boutari) is made from grapes grown on 30-year-old vines on the century-old Matsa Estate in Kanza, a delightful oasis within the urban sprawl of modern Athens.

Savatiano is the most widely planted wine grape in Attica today.

The photo is from *Ampelography* by Manolis N. Stavrakakis, Tropi Publications, Athens (in Greek), and is used with the kind permission of the author.

Savatiano also blends well with the brighter and more acidic **Assyrtiko** (originally from the Cyclades) or **Moscophilero** (originally from the Peloponnesos), both of which are now being grown in Attica. Blends of Savatiano and Roditis (see below), in which the Savatiano is the major element, are widely available in Athenian restaurants and tavernas. Look for **Domaine Evharis** (70% / 30%) or **Apelia Dry White** (60% /40%), among others. The bulk of the Savatiano produced in Athens, however, is still used to make retsina where the grape's lack of acidity can be masked by the addition of the resin.

Malagousia (Ma-la-goo-ZYA) is an interesting white grape that was first recognized in the region around Nafpaktos in western Greece. In the 1970s it was included in a mix of little known varietals that were being grown experimentally by Prof. Logothetis of the University of Thessalonica, on a vineyard owned by Domaine Carras. There, winemaker Evangelos Gerovassiliou recognized the grape's potential and, in the 1990s, crafted a barrel of 100% Malagousia wine that literally brought the grape back from the brink of extinction. As a single-varietal wine, Malagousia is full-bodied and very aromatic (jasmine and mint). For an excellent example try the one produced by Roxani Matsa who has been named Wine Personality of the Year by the Association of Greek Wine Journalists for her preservation of traditional winemaking.

Roditis (Rho-THEE-tis) is not the name of a single grape varietal but rather an umbrella term that is used for several different, but closely related, clones that are grouped together by the common "pinkish" skin that the name (Greek *rodos* = rose) implies. The multi-clonal nature of the grape explains the great diversity in the character of the wines that carry that grape's name, which can be traced back at least to the 2nd century CE. Unoaked Roditis wines are lighter than oaked versions, and present a clean and crisp wine with a lemon zest nose and citrus and/or green pear on the palate. It is a great wine to enjoy as an aperitif, or as an accompaniment to a selection of Greek appetizers (*mezédhes*).

A Regional Specialty

Many visitors to Greece mistakenly believe that Retsina—which they often compare to turpentine—is synonymous with all Greek wine, but this distinctive wine is more precisely associated with Athens and its hinterlands. In fact, the Greek government has awarded it a special "Appellation by Tradition" in order to recognize that fact and protect the product.

This use of resins in the winemaking process is several millennia old. Traces of terebinth resin (*Pistacia atlantica*) have been identified in ceramic wine jars at several ancient sites in the eastern Mediterranean, including the Greek island of Crete. Resin kills bacteria (especially the acetobacter) and thus it was added directly to the wine as a preservative. It was also used to seal wine containers. This would keep out oxygen and prevent or retard the transformation of the nticipated wine into a less welcome ·inegar. Although today's resinated vines might be considered to be an ıcquired taste, several ancient authors vrote eloquently on the niceties of ısing specific resins, just as modern Chardonnay aficionados might discuss he relative merits of French, American, r Slovenian oak. Pliny, writing n the 1st century CE, considered erebinth resin to be the "best and nost eloquent" of all, while most nodern vintners tend to champion he Aleppo Pine (*Pinus halepensis*).

The iconic yellow label of a bottle of Kourtaki Retsina.
Photo by Nsaa (Wikimedia Commons, CC BY-SA 3.0).

Historically in Athens, retsina has been nade in large wooden casks, often n the same taverna or restaurant in vhich the wine would eventually be erved. There the owner would flavor he must (usually Savatiano and/ r Roditis) with varying amounts of nastic or pine resin, and fermentation vould proceed in-house. In the 960s retsina began to be bottled ommercially and today the buyer ıas a wide selection of brands from which to choose. Internationally, the most opularly selling retsina is the Kourtaki brand, Retsina of Attica, made by the Kourtakis family which has a history of over a century of winemaking in the rea. It uses one hundred percent Savatiano grapes that are grown on Mt. Parnes nd is easily recognizable either by its crown cap or its iconic yellow label.

)ne of the first to experiment with making this classic wine appeal to a wider udience was Giannis Paraskevopoulos of Gaia Winery. Called **Ritinitis Nobilis**, t is produced from one hundred percent Roditis grown in the Agialia area outhwest of Attica to which is added a minimal amount of resin (*Pinus halepensis*). 'he result is a wine that is surprisingly light, well balanced (citrus vs. pine), and ery drinkable, with an alcohol level under 12 percent. From Attica itself, try the etsina made at Domaine Papagiannakos from 100% Savatiano grapes grown on fty year old vines near the suburb of Markopoulo (Mesogeia Appellation), or **nodos** by Domaine Euinos in the village of Spata. Incidentally, Plato, by the ·ay, used the word *anodos* to describe the path to enlightenment (*Republic* IV).

Vhichever end of the retsina spectrum you choose, to really appreciate this ational treasure, it must be taken well chilled and with food: Greek food! There is

Brettos. The best place to taste wine in Athens. The lights will draw you in, but the wine will make you stay—plus its very enthusiastic and knowledgeable staff.
Photo courtesy of the Time Traveling Gourmet.

something special about the way that the flavors of a well-made retsina develop and compliment a grilled country sausage or an intensely flavored eggplant mousaka.

Celebrate!

Historically, the grapes of Attica have not been used for making sparkling wines, probably because the heat of the Attic plain is not conducive to growing grapes varietals that hold their acid well. But, if your visit coincides with a personal celebration, pick up a bottle of **EVA**, a semi-sparkling *vin pétillant* made by the Charmat ("closed tank") method from Roditis and Moscophilero grapes that are grown on the slopes of Mt. Gerania near Attica's border with Megara. It is a fresh and fruity wine with fine, long lasting bubbles (*mousse*). The Evharis Estate also makes a variety of other sparklers from interesting blends of international varieties.

Wine Bars & Bottle Shops

Brettos was founded in 1909 by Michael Brettos, a distiller. It is housed in a 200-year-old building in the heart of the Plaka at Odos Kydatheneion 41, near its intersection with Odos Adrianou (Odos = "street"). They offer about 100 Greek wines by the glass, 40 fruit-flavored (Smyrna-style) liquors ranging from amoretto to watermelon, as well as brandies, beers, and even a genuine French absinthe that is 55% alcohol by volume!

They also serve a large selection of Greek cocktails, including the "Zorba" which is made from ouzo, orange juice, grenadine, and Blue Curacao. Frankly, it is difficult to envision Anthony Quinn and Blue Curacao in the same room. Perhaps calling it the "Alan Bates" would be better? Better stick with the wine!

Most visits to Athens include a viewing of the changing of the guard in front of the Tomb of the Unknown Soldier on Syntagma (Constitution) Square in the heart of the city. Fortunately, after the performance is over, the visitor is in striking distance of two very good wine shops.

The Choragic (Choral) Monument of Lysicrates.

Cellier (Odos Kriezotou 1) is a very sophisticated wine shop situated just off the northeastern corner of Syntagma. An upscale wine merchant that has been in business since 1938, Cellier carries an excellent selection of quality Greek and international wines, many of which are featured in their own monthly magazine. *Wine Story* (at Odos Nikis 21) is a more pedestrian shop located off the southwestern corner of the square. Although its sign identifies it as a "Delicatessen" it is really a wine shop with a wide selection of local Greek varietals and vintages. What sets the Wine Story apart, however, is the fact that you can also buy bulk wine that is sold by weight, just as it was in the old days. Bring your own container or use one of theirs and then get down to the decision process, choosing from about ten different varietals, some of which are certified bio-organic. Or, while in the Plaka, visit *Finewine* (Odos Lisikratous 3) located directly across from the monument erected by a wealthy Athenian in celebration of his financial support of a play in the Theater of Dionysos that was awarded first prize *c.* 335 BCE.

Sweet Tooth

Sweets in Athens can vary from the traditional "spoon sweets" of the rustic Athenian countryside to the sophisticated creations of world-renowned chocolatiers.

In the not too distant past, a visitor to an Athenian home, whether the next-door neighbor or a weary traveler from afar, would have been proudly offered a welcoming treat (*kérasma*) designed to refresh and reenergize the guest. These were thick, colorful fruit preserves (cherry, mandarin, fig, etc.), usually home-made, and were presented in the bowl of a spoon submerged in a tall glass of cool water. Today, commercially produced spoon sweets are available in most Athenian supermarkets and they can be good, but do keep an eye out for smaller brands like Idiston that are made—without preservatives—in small batches, as they have been made in Athenian kitchens for centuries.

For something more elaborate, head for Odos Karagiorgi Servias at the northwest corner of Syntagma Square. There, on the block between Odos Nikis and Odos Voulis, are several shops that will appeal to any sweet tooth. Start with *Leonidas*, a Belgian chocolatier with a Greek name that has been supplying Athens and the rest of the world with its famous pralines since 1913. Equally tasty treats are available at *Kava Poton*, *Le Chocolat*, and *Aristokrateion*: all located within a few doors of each other.

Wine Words to Watch For

O.P.A.P. (Translation: "Appellation of Superior Quality" - cf. the French V.Q.P.R.D. (*Vin de Qualité Produit dans des Régions Déterminées*). Indicates and regulates specific terroir, viticultural programs, and/or vinicultural practices. Additional refinements include:

- Reserve: 2–3 years of combined (cask and bottle) aging
- Grand Reserve: 3–4 years of combined (cask and bottle) aging

TOPIKOS OINOS (Translation: "Local Wine" or "Regional Wine"- cf. the French *Vin de Pays*). An appellation with less stringent regulations that is used by many winemakers as a "stepping stone" towards O.P.A.P. status. Additional terminology includes:

- *Ktima* – Domaine or Estate
- *Monastiri* – Monastery
- *Archondiko* – Chateau

EPITRAPEZIOS OINOS (Translation: "Table Wine" - cf. the French *Vin de Table*). Not necessarily the lowest category in quality as it is used by some winemakers to avoid the constrictions required of the other appellations. Additional terminology includes:

- *Kava* – ("cellared") – 2–3 years of combined (cask and bottle) aging.

Cheers!

In Athens,
just say

YIA-sou!

("to your health")

Barcelona

Catalonia, Spain

a Basilica de la Sagrada Familia (Church of the Holy Family)—Antonio Gaudí's masterpiece of Iodernism—is Barcelona's most striking landmark. Begun in 1883, this UNESCO World Heritage te is still under construction. Photo by rheins (Wikimedia Commons, CC BY 3.0).

Travel through the Roman province of Hispania was always dusty, and very often dangerous. Nowhere was this truer than the section of the Via Augusta that ran between Narbo (modern Narbonne) and the old Phoenician seaport t Taraco (modern Tarragona). Here the road swung inland through the lands of ie Laietani clinging to the hills and avoiding marshy, and potentially malarial, tretches along the coast. But there was a bright spot: a small garrison on Mont aber, the low extension of the waterless Montjuïc massif. Here one could rest, shed ie burdens of travel, and enjoy the freshest of seafood—especially the legendary ysters—washed down with the hearty wines of the Laietanian hinterland.

Augustus, adopted son of Julius Caesar and first Roman Emperor (27 BCE–14 CE), was deified by the Senate after his death and worshipped as such in the forum at Barcino.

Metropolitan Museum of Arts (99.35.6), a gift of Joseph H. Durkee, 1899 (CCO 1.0).

his small settlement was Barkeno (spellings vary), a name possibly derived rom that of the Carthaginian general Hamilcar Barca, Hannibal's father, 'ho had occupied the area briefly toward the end of the 3rd century BCE. To ie Romans, however, it was the *Colonia Faventia Julia Augusta Pia Barcino,* ›rtunately shortened to Barcino by the Emperor Augustus around the year 15.

Barcino was good to Rome, sending gold, silver, wine, grain, and fish sauce back to the capital. And, in turn, Rome was kind to the little settlement. Emperor Tiberius graced its forum with a temple dedicated to the deified Augustus, resplendent with Corinthian columns over nine meters high. Life was good, but it wouldn't last. As the weakness of the central administration radiated out to the fringes of the empire, Emperor Claudius II (reigned 268–270) was forced to raise Barcino's walls to a height of over eight meters. But this only slowed the inevitable and the local economy continued to sink into decline

During the late 4th and 5th centuries, a variety of Germanic (Gothic) tribes, including the notorious Vandals and Visigoths, took advantage of the situation and slipped southward through the filter of the Pyrenees where they settled down, gradually adopting both the trappings and substance of the Hispanic-Roman culture. Surprisingly, life in Visigothic Hispania was one of culture. Art, architecture and literature flourished.

To the south, however, storm clouds were gathering. In 711, Tariq Ibn Ziyad and his army crossed the Strait of Gibraltar and drove northward, taking what would become known as *Barchinona* just six years later. For the next 80 years it would be directly under the thumb of the Caliph of Cordoba, a part of *al-Andalus* ("The Paradise") as the invaders referred to the portions of the Iberian Peninsula under their control.

A mosaic of the Three Graces decorated the floor of a 3rd–4th century Roman villa in Barcelona.
Museu d'Arquelogia de Catalunya (Barcelona), accession no. 19019 (Public domain).

Eventually Charlemagne's son, Louis the Pius, reclaimed most of the land north of the Ebro River, including Barcelona in 801, and turned it into a series of small counties (the *Marca Hispanica*) designed to serve as a buffer between Moslems and Christians. Although quasi-independent, the *marca* were usually under the control of the Count of Barcelona, a title that was made hereditary by William the Hairy (Guifré el Pelás) when he held the position from 878–897.

Over the centuries Barcelona has suffered more than its share of pestilence and plague, especially the Back Death. During the first outbreak (1348–1351) it is estimated that 40% of the city's population died, and it may have been the impetus for the construction of two of the most beautiful churches in the city: Santa Maria del Mar and Santa Maria del Pi. Both are striking examples of the soaring Catalan Gothic style.

With the marriage of Isabella I of Castile to Ferdinand II of Aragon in 1469, and the subsequent discovery of the Americas, the economic interests of the Iberian Peninsula shifted away from the Mediterranean and to the Atlantic. Barcelona's economy began to falter again, a situation made worse by Catalonia's complete loss of autonomy after the Battle of Barcelona brought the Wars of the Spanish Succession to an unhappy end in 1714.

During the 19th century, fueled by prosperity generated by the Industrial Revolution, Barcelona enjoyed an economic and cultural renaissance *(La Renaixença)* whose symbol was appropriately the Phoenix rising from the flames. In 1856 the medieval city walls were torn down and the city was allowed to expand, ultimately leading to the architectural explosion known as *Modernisme* made famous by Antonio Gaudí, Joseph Puig i Cadafalsch, and others.

After Tariq Ibn Zayid brought his army across the Strait of Gibraltar he burned his ships to preclude retreat, saying that he had come either to conquer or to perish.
(Gibraltar £5 banknote (detail). Printer, de la Rue, 1995).

Barcelona's suffering during the Spanish Civil War (1936–1939) was observed first hand by George Orwell and vividly presented in *Homage to Catalonia.* Less than a year after Hitler rained havoc on tiny Guernica, Barcelona suffered days of deadly bombing by Mussolini's air force in support of Gen. Francisco Franco's "Nationalist" forces. On January 26th, 1939, Franco marched into Barcelona and declared total victory. The Generalissimo would rule Spain as a dictator until his death in 1975 at the age of 82. He was the longest ruling dictator in modern European history.

But the phoenix would rise again. Two days after Franco's death, Juan Carlos I was crowned King of Spain, retaining ("by grace of God") the millennia-old title: Count of Barcelona. As has been the case so often in the past, the relationship between Catalonia and the Crown remains a rocky one today, but progress is being made despite the fact that calls for self-determination always seem to be simmering—just below the surface.

The Grapes Of Cava

Cava (KA-va) is *the* wine of Barcelona, and refers specifically to a sparkling wine made by the *méthode traditionelle* in which secondary fermentation (the one that produces the bubbles) takes place in the bottle. Often referred to simply as "Spanish Champagne" (*champan, champaña, Xampany,* etc.), the word Cava ("cave" or "cellar") was adopted in 1970 at the insistence of the EU in order to distinguish it from similarly crafted wines from the French Champagne region. But there is more than a nominal difference. Whereas the three major grape varieties used in Champagne are Chardonnay, Pinot Noir, and Meunier, Cava utilizes three Spanish (actually Catalonian) varieties: Macabeo, Parellada, and Xarello. And, while Spanish DO (*Denominación de Origen*) regulations allow Cava to be produced in several areas, Catalonian Penedès makes about 95% of all of the Cava presently produced.

Cava was born in Sant Sadurní d'Anoia, a few miles west of Barcelona, where the famous Codorníu, Freixenet, and Gramona houses are located. Here in the 1870s, José Raventós of Codorníu began experimenting with sparkling wines after a trip to Rheims/Épernay. Later, when phylloxera swept through France, he was ready—with the help of the new and rapidly expanding rail industry—to meet the demands of the international market. And, when the disease eventually struck the vineyards of Spain, they were replanted with the three canonical Cava grapes, grafted onto more disease-resistant North American rootstock, resulting in the popular beverage that we enjoy today.

WHITE GRAPES

Three white grapes are considered to be the Holy Trinity of Cava, the blending of which, and the percentages of each, will dictate the individual characteristics of a specific wine.

Xarello or Xarel-lo (Sha-RAIL-loh) is a pale, thick-skinned grape of relatively local origin that is high in sugar with medium to high acid (think Granny Smith apple). Although it provides the framework upon which the other two Cava grapes are hung, it also makes an interesting wine on its own. **Creu de Lavit** by Segura Viudas is a still wine made completely from the juice of hand-harvested Xarello grapes that are fermented in oak to add a subtle smokiness to the base flavors of apricot and ripe pear. Recaredo makes an excellent 100% Xarello Cava from a vineyard planted in 1940. Hands-on attention to every detail, combined with long aging *sur lees*, limits production to fewer than 3000—individually numbered—bottles a year.

The thick-skinned Xarello grape is one of the three traditional grapes of Cava.
Photo by Marimar Estate, courtesy of Familia Torres.

Macabeo (Mah-kah-BAY-oh) is another thick-skinned, heat-resistant grape that has been planted widely across northern Spain for centuries. Although possibly related genetically to Xarello, it may ultimately be shown to possess a Middle Eastern pedigree. Slightly floral and fruity, with low–medium acidity, it is usually the dominant grape in Cava.

The individual characteristics of Macabeo are most easily encountered in the white wines of the Rioja DO where the grape is known as **Viura**. However, keep an eye out for wines from L'Olivera, a Catalonian cooperative whose members, self-described as "people with difficulties," participate in the entire process. Their **Agaliu** (quite dry) and **Missenyora** (with some residual sugar) are both mono-cépage Macabeo wines that are fermented in oak and allowed to sit on the lees until spring.

Parellada (Par-eh-LYAH-dah) is a fruity, aromatic grape that grows vigorously along the Ebro River to the west of Barcelona. Although blended to add its acidity and a degree of freshness to Cava, the grape also makes a very good wine on its wn. Gramona's semi-sparkling **Moustillant Blanc Brut**, made from 100% Parellada emonstrates the citrus (grapefruit) flavors of the grape, while single varietal, still 'ines such as Miguel Torres' **Viña Sol** and **San Valentín** tend to evoke (ripe) stone 'uits that intensify when served at temperatures above the recommended 8C/46F.

RED GRAPES

ava can also come in color: the pale, salmon-pink color of a Cava Rosado. Several rape varieties are allowed in its production: **Garnacha** (AKA Grenache or 'ernaccia), **Monastrell** (AKA Mourvèdre), or **Pinot Noir** being used by most of ne major houses. But the mysterious **Trepat** can also be used. Grown mostly in ne Conca de Barberá, just inland from Penedès, it adds vibrant color and hints f red-berried fruitiness (and some say cinnamon) to the blend. Two excellent)0% Trepat Cava are made by Agustí Torelló Mata: **Rosat Trepat Brut** packaged ı standard 750 ml bottles and **Bayanno Rosat** that is available in 375ml bottles.

CAVA

SIX DEGREES OF SWEETNESS

DRY

Brut Nature

Brut

Brut Reserve

Sec/Seco

Semisec/Semiseco

Dolsec/Dulce

SWEET

Celebrate!

hoosing a celebratory beverage in a land where sparkling wines are commonplace an be a challenge. So why not break with tradition and try a sweet passito from ne **Malvasia Sitges** grape, a rare and distinctive member of the Malvasia amily, grown in a small (6 acre) vineyard at the Hospital de Saint Juan Bautista e Sitges, just 20 miles SW of Barcelona. Produced and marketed y volunteers in order to support the hospital, the grape 'as brought to the area originally by Spanish mercenaries eturning home in the 13th–14th centuries. At one time close) extinction, the grape's survival is due to the generosity of Ianuel Llopis de Casades who willed his small vineyard to the ospital provided that they would continue to make the wine.

, however, only a sparkler will do, try to find a bottle of Vega de ibes' **Ancestral**, made by a technique that is thought to predate e méthode traditionelle. Here the juice of the Malvasia Sitges rapes is fermented in chestnut barrels, cooled, and bottled 'hile the wine is dormant. Then the temperature is raised and e fermentation is completed without the need for dosage. lightly sweet, while retaining the acidity of the grape, **Ancestral** oes very well with a box of celebratory Spanish chocolate.

Pere Romeu at *Els Quatre Gats* restaurant/pub, the home of Bohemian Barcelona. Color lithograph by Ramón Casas. Google Art Project (PD).

Wine Bars & Bottle Shops

lthough it can be difficult to find, *Els Quatre Gats* (at Carrer Iontsio 3 bis) is definitely worth the search. Housed in the Casa Iartí, designed and built by Modernist architect Joseph Puig i adafalsch in 1897, it was the brainchild of painter Pere Romeu who was inspired by the famous Parisian cabaret *Le Chat Noir*. It served as a place of refreshment, conversation, and entertainment for some of the most famous artists of the day, including Antonio Gaudí, Joan Miró, and a teen-age Pablo Picasso. This is the perfect place to enjoy an array of Catalan specialties, or simply to sip a cold glass of Cava while drinking in the spirit of *Modernisme*.

And if you are in search of something to bring back to the ship, go directly to the *Vila Viniteca* in the Bari Gótic (Carrers Agullers 7) where it has been since 1932. With estimated holdings of between 4000 and 7000 bottles and a very helpful multi-lingual staff, you are sure to find something that you like. They also own the gourmet food shop at no. 9, which is also a must.

Images of Darth Vader and BB-8, from the award winning Star Wars sculpture (in chocolate) by Xavi Clopés, appear on the wrapper of the edible ticket to Barcelona's *Museu de la Xocolata*.
Photo courtesy of the Time Traveling Gourmet.

Sweet Tooth

Barcelona has enjoyed a love affair with chocolate ever since it was brought home from the "New World" five centuries ago. After all, Salvador Dalí claimed that his favorite dish was lobster with chocolate sauce. So why not visit the *Museu de la Xocolata* (Carrer del Comerc 36). It is a celebration of all things chocolate and takes you on a journey from the growing and processing of the cacao pods to their transformation into a tempting array of mouth-watering confections, many of which are available for purchase in the gift shop. Along the way you will be treated to a variety of chocolate sculptures that range from a somber *Pietà* by Michelangelo to a whimsical tableaux of Asterix & Obelix. And don't lose your ticket! It is an individually numbered bar of extra fine chocolate (minimum 73% cacao).

Cheers!

In Barcelona,
just say

Çanakkale

Turkey

The Wooden Horse from the 2005 film *Troy*, a gift to Çanakkale from the film's star Brad Pitt, is an instant and constant reminder of the area's long association with Homer's Troy. Photo by Pmk58 (Wikimedia Commons, CC BY-SA 4.0).

Maritime gateway to the fabled walls of Homer's Troy, Çanakkale was born behind rugged defenses built by Sultan Mehmet the Conqueror shortly after he stormed Constantinople in the year 1453.

The head of the wine-god Dionysos, crowned with a wreath of ivy, appears on a mid-4th century BCE gold *stater* from Lampsakos (modern Lapseki) in the district of Çanakkale. *Cabinet des Médailles*, Paris. Photo by Marie-Lan Nguyen (Wikimedia Commons, CC BY 2.5).

Located at the narrowest point of the Dardanelles (Hellespont) close to the ancient Greek town of Lampsakos, this *Kale Sultaniye* ("Fortress of the Sultan"), together with its sister-fortress on the European shore, was designed to protect against the marauding Venetian navy. Historically they have provided a bulwark against any hostile ship bound for the Sea of Marmara, the Golden Horn, or the Black Sea beyond.

Although this area has been inhabited since at least the Chalcolithic Period—over 5000 years ago—it was with the epic tradition of the 8th century BCE, especially in the *Iliad* and the *Odyssey*, that things slowly began to come into historical focus. Homer's audiences were well aware that Jason and the crew of the *Argo* had sailed these waters on their way to retrieve the Golden Fleece. And most would have remembered that one of these Argonauts, Nestor of Pylos, had returned with ninety black-hulled ships to support the combined Greek effort to bring the comely Helen back from Troy (*Iliad* II.581ff.).

A fragment of wall decoration from Xerxes' Palace at Persepolis (Iran) depicting a royal guardsman in procession, 486–465 BCE.
Cleveland Museum of Art. CCO 1.O Universal Public Domaine Dedication.

Later, it was the Persians' turn to cross the Hellespont, to avenge Athens for supporting several Ionian cities that had risen up in revolt. Here, the Persian King Darius is said to have gained an appreciation for the excellent wines of the area while preparing his fleet for a maritime expedition to punish these impudent Greeks. Unfortunately his plans were dashed at the Battle of Marathon in 490 BCE and his fleet returned home in shambles. Ten years later his son, Xerxes I, attempted to settle the score by linking hundreds of his ships together (bow-to-stern) to bridge the Hellespont. After a storm destroyed the project, Xerxes ordered his soldiers to administer lashings to the waters and to brand them with hot irons (Herodotus, *Histories* VII: 33–58). He then rebuilt the bridges (this time with the prows facing into the current), and moved his army across. He was off to Thermopylae and the eventual destruction of Athens.

And it didn't end with Xerxes. In 334 BCE Alexander the Great crossed these waters with more than 12,000 soldiers on their way to pay homage at the Tomb of Achilles before moving inland to rid the world of tyranny. And, while they were at it, to repay the Persians for the humiliating destruction that they had inflicted earlier upon the city of Athens.

Hecamede, a young serving girl from the island of Tenedos, prepares *kykeon*, a special wine cocktail, for Nestor of Pylos who was said to be the wisest of all the Greeks who had assembled beneath the walls of Troy (*Iliad* XI: 624–35). The "Iliupersis Cup", a Red-figure *kylix* by Brygos, *c.* 490 BCE.
Musée du Louvre (G152), The Bammerville Collection, 1881 (PD).

Century after century it has gone this way: back and forth, back and forth. Mighty armies marching east then west, always driven by the loftiest of intentions. So it was that five hundred years after the founding of Çanakkale these waters foiled the plans of a young Winston Churchill. Then First Lord of the British Admiralty, he tried to force "the Narrows" with disastrous results for the Allies. On a single day in March of 1915, the French dreadnaught *Bouvet* and British battleships *Irresistible* and *Ocean* were sent to the bottom of the Dardanelles. This precipitated the equally disastrous British and ANZAC landings on the adjacent Gallipoli *(Gelibolu)* Peninsula, a move that would eventually bring about the creation of the modern Turkish State.

..ocal Grape Varieties

..lajor Turkish wine houses such as Doluca, Kutman, and Sevilen offer a variety of ..ood wines crafted from both Turkish and international grape varieties, but a visit .. a small port such as Çanakkale gives one the opportunity to taste wines made ..om grapes that are either indigenous to the area or that have been grown there for ..enturies.

..everal such grapes are grown on the island of Bozcaada (Boz-DJA-a-dah), ancient ..enedos, just off the coast of Çanakkale province. The Greek historian Herodotus ..aimed that the gods had created Bozcaada simply so that people could live longer, ..hile the ancient Egyptian *bon vivant,* Athenaeus of Naukratis, praised the flavor of ..s marjoram as well as the beauty of its women. It was the Trojan War, however, that ..rought the most fame to Tenedos. The island was sacred to Apollo, the god who had ..ent the plague that had ravaged the Greek camp at the opening of Homer's *Iliad.* ..ehind its heights the Greeks had hidden their fleet after leaving a tempting Wooden ..orse in front of the walls of Troy, thus prompting Poseidon's priest Laocoön to utter ..s famous warning about gift-bearing Greeks (Virgil, *Aeneid* II: 60–70). And it was ..om that same island that giant serpents came to attack Laocoön and his sons in ..der to avenge his meddling in plans that only the gods should be allowed to make.

..VHITE GRAPES

..avuş (Cha-VUSH) is considered by many to be the finest of Turkey's ..any table grape varieties but, surprisingly, it can also make a very ..ubstantial, food-friendly wine. Corvus Winery's **Teneia** (Ten-NAY-ya), ..ade from 100% Çavuş, is a pale yellow wine with white floral aromas. It .. very clean and crisp on the palate with a slightly mineral finish.

..asilaki (Vas-i-LAH-ki), a grape whose name suggests a Greek origin, has ..nall, round, yellow berries with a slight greenish tinge. Both Talay and Corvus **..eleia** Series) make low acid, low alcohol (often 12%) wines from 100% Vasilaki ..apes grown on Bozcaada. Corvus also sun dries a small percentage of its ..asilaki grapes to make a *passito*. This technique of drying the fruit to raise ..ugar levels and concentrate flavors can be traced back into deepest antiquity ..d a side-by-side tasting of these two wines is both enjoyable and instructive.

..asilaki is also used as a blending wine. Talay's **Assos White** is an interesting ..arriage of Vasilaki and the little known (and difficult to document) **..dalan** grape grown to the south of Çanakkale. However, Corvus' **Karga ..eyaz** ("White Crow"), a blend of Vasilaki and Çavuş that is intentionally ..afted for "the young palate" is best avoided. It opens with a disappointing ..tringency that improves only slightly with exposure to air.

..ultaniye (Sul-TAN-i-yeh), with clusters of oval, pale-green berries, was ..aditionally grown throughout the Ottoman Empire for consumption as raisins ..*ultanas*). Outside Turkey, the Sultaniye/Sultana grape is more widely known as

According to Greek mythology, Leander swam the Hellespont nightly to visit his lover Hero, a priestess of Aphrodite/Venus, who guided him to her with a lamp. One stormy night the light blew out, Leander drowned and, in her grief, Hero threw herself into the raging sea. The tragedy was commemorated on the coinage of several Roman emperors and even by Lord Byron when he swam the strait himself in 1810.

Each year the Çanakkale Rotary Club also celebrates the event with the Dardanelles Strait Swimming Competition on August 30th, the anniversary of the final Turkish victory in their War of Independence in 1922.

Evelyn de Morgan, *Hero Holding the Beacon for Leander* (*c.* 1885), The Athenaeum (PD).

Local Izmir grapes are very popular and readily available in the weekly, open air food market *(Balgat Pazarı)* in Cankaya, Ankara, Turkey.
Photo by E4024 (Wikimedia Commons, CC BY-SA 4.0).

the Thompson Seedless after William Thompson, a grower in California's Central Valley. Both varieties may be related to the rounder-berried **Kismis** grape that was also widely grown for raisins throughout the Ottoman Empire. Büyülübağ (Bew-yew-lew-BAH) Winery makes an aromatic and fruity (green apple and citrus) wine from hand-selected clusters of Sultaniya grapes in Turkey's first gravity-flow winery, located on Avaş Island in the Sea of Marmara just a few miles north of Çanakkale.

RED GRAPES

Karasakız (KA-ra SAH-kez) is a local, thin-skinned grape that is predominantly used to produce rosé wines with soft tannins. Thes wines are best served chilled and are often enjoyed as an aperitif. Melen Winery offers a 100% Karasakız Rosé in their **Ganohora** Series that has the aroma of grenadine and the flavors of summer fruits. Talay's **Halikarnas Blush** presents a medium dry wine with a similar profile. Talay's **Troya Red** and Corvus' **Vinium** Series blends Karasakız with **Karalahna** (KA-ra LAH-na), a grape that is very closely related to the Xynomavro of Greece, to produce light, ruby colored wines with red currant flavors and soft tannins.

In this manner wine-filed amphoras *(amphorae)* were stacked aboard ships and traded the length and breadth of the Mediterranean. Bodrum Museum of Underwater Archaeology (Bodrum Castle), Turkey.
Photo by Ad Meskens (Wikimedia Commons, CC BY-SA 3.0).

Kuntra (KUN-tra), a grape that is naturally high in sugar, will easily yield a wine with an alcohol level of (or over) 15%. Historically it has been used extensively in the Turkish "cognac" industry as well as to make low quality dessert wines. Talay's **Kuntra Sweet**, with a fair exposure to oak, is one of the better examples of the second category. A better choice might be the Kuntra released by Corvus in their **Aegea** (Eg-Gay-ya) series. It is a dark, ruby colored wine with good structure and medium tannins. Kuntra is also blended with the Karalahna grape by both Talay and Corvus, while the latter adds a third component, Cabernet Sauvignon, to its **Kırmızı Karga** ("Red Crow"). This is another of their wines that is intentionally blended to appeal to "the young palate."

Adakarası (A-da-KA-ra-seh), "Island Black," is also indigenous to Avşa island. When well made, its large, thick-skinned berries will deliver a soft, deep-red wine redolent with blackberry and dark stone fruits. Often with alcohol levels as low as 12%, wines from this grape make a great companion for a summer lunch along the humid Anatolian coast. Büyülübağ Winer demonstrates the versatility of the Adakarası grape. Its **Iris** (ee-REES) **Rosé**, made from hand-harvested and hand-sorted fruit, is an attractive pink wine exhibiting strawberry and raspberry on the nose and other early summer fruits on the palate. Büyülübağ **Iris Rosé** may be difficult to pronounce but it is easy to find since it is marketed in colorful, elaborately decorated bottles that stand out on any shelf.

Papazkarası (Papa-KA-ra-seh), meaning "Priest's Black" or "Black Bishop," has large, round, thick-skinned berries. Traditionally it has been used both as a table grape and a wine grape, and is often said to express more of the *terroir* of its European heritage than do the wines of the Anatolian soils and climates across the Dardanelles. Unfortunately, the grape is on the road to extinction unless major efforts are made to save it soon. One winery that is making such an effort is Melen Wines, owned by a family with a deep sense of the history of the region, who call their **Papazkarası Reserve** "the forgotten Thracian prince." Made from 100% Papazkarası, and given a touch of oak, it offers the intense flavor of dark stone fruits beneath a light canopy of vanilla. Kutman's **Özel Kav Papazkarası** is also recommended but it is not easy to find.

Wine Words to Watch For

Wine – Şarap

Wine shop – Şarap Evi

White – Beyaz

Red - Kırmızı

Dry – Sek

A frieze from the 6th century BCE Temple of Athena at Assos (modern Behramkale), south of Çanakkale, celebrates the conviviality typified by the classical *symposium*.

Paris, Musée du Louvre (MA2829), gift of Sultan Mahmud II, 1838 (Wikimedia Commons, PD).

Celebrate!

When only a glass of "the bubbly" will suffice, look for one of Kutman's sparkling wines that are made, in what they refer to as the "traditional" method, from local grapes grown near their winery in Mürefte (ancient Myriophyton) on the SE shores of the Sea of Marmara. Called **Feyzi Kutman Köpüren**, it can be either straw-colored or pale pink depending on whether it is made from their Semillon or Papazkarası grapes.

Poseidon's serpents attack Laocoön and his sons for having dared to warn the Trojans against Greeks bearing gifts. Said to be the work of three sculptors from Rhodes, it most probably dates to the 1st century BCE.

Musei Vaticani: Museo Pio-Clementino (1506): Inv. 1059, 1064, 1067 (Wikimedia Commons, PD).

Wine Bars & Bottle Shops

There are several shops near Çanakkale's ferry port where several of these local wines can be tried and a bottle or two brought back to the ship. Keep an eye out for signs proclaiming a *Şarap Evi* (Wine House) such as that at 18 Mart Caddesi 77 or the one at Kayserili Ahmet Paşa 42. Unfortunately, many cruise ships now use the larger port to the south of Çanakkale and shore time by the harbor—if any—is often quite limited.

In Istanbul things are easier. *Corvus Wine & Bite* at Şair Nedim Caddesi 5 in the Beşiktaş neighborhood is the brainchild of Corvus' founder, Turkish architect Resit Soley, who for the past several years has worked tirelessly to bring back the Cavuş, Kuntra, and Karalahna grapes on Bozcaada Island. The Corvus Wine & Bite is a veritable celebration of the island's wines that can be enjoyed with, or without, a selection of imaginative and well-paired small plates. Difficult to find even for taxi drivers, Şair Nedim is off Süleyman Seba Caddesi and runs along the downhill side of the W Hotel.

Sweet Tooth

Colorful Turkish Delight, *Lokum,* crafted from a seemingly endless palette of flowers, fruits, spices, and nuts is readily available in Çanakkale, but one of the favorite sweets of the local residents is *peynir helva(sı):* a rich, golden blend of sheep's milk cheese, egg yolks, semolina, and sugar. Served warm, at room temperature, or cool it is delicious. Two very good places to enjoy it are both located on Yalı Caddesi: try either *Babalık Peynir Helvası* at no. 47 or *Husmenoğlu* at no. 29. The latter shop has been there since 1912.

Çanakkale (Cha-NA-ka-leh) derives its name from the Turkish *Çanak Kalesı* ("Fortress of the Pottery Vases), recalling its reputation for the production of fine ceramics. The province of Çanakkale includes the small, offshore islands of Bozcaada (ancient Tenedos) and Gökçeada (ancient Imbros), as well as parts of the Gallipoli peninsula on the European side of the strait. Together with the contiguous province of Tekirdağ on the western shores of the Sea of Marmara, they formed one of the most prolific grape-growing areas throughout antiquity, and today they account for about 40% of total Turkish wine production.

Pronunciation: The phonetic suggestions offered here are approximate and were worked out with the help of Mr. Taylan Sargin of the Sensus Wine Boutique in the Amenon Galata Hotel (Istanbul) to whom the author is extremely grateful. The pronunciation of Turkish words can be tricky. Watch out especially for the un-dotted I/ı (pronounced "eh") and the Ğ/ğ (that is not pronounced at all but rather lengthens the vowel in the preceding syllable).

Civitavecchia

Port of Rome, Italy

he fortress completed by Michelangelo in 1537 still welcomes visitors to the Port of Civitavecchia,
the Province of Rome, in the Region of Lazio, Italy.
oto by Olaf Meister (Wikimedia Commons, CC BY-SA 4.0).

What drew Bronze Age settlers to these shores more than 5000 years ago may never be known. It may have been easy access to the mineral wealth of the Tolfa Mountains or the pleasures offered by the thermal springs 1at bubbled up nearby. But the rich—and tasty—sea life lurking in the coastal waters the Tyrrhenian Sea cannot be dismissed as the reason that they stayed. For stay ey did!

The Roman Emperor Trajan, who ruled from 98 to 117, began the work of enlarging the harbor that continues to the present day.
Photo courtesy of Paul Sherman, WPClipart.

ater, while bronze tools were giving way to those of iron, the ethnic composition of e population was also changing as those who would become known as "Etruscans" egan to take up residence. Slowly, during the 7th and 6th centuries BCE, the small uts of the early pioneers were replaced with much more substantial structures.

hese must have been heady days for the people of the coast as sporadic visits y Phoenician traders became a steady stream of the Greek merchants who ould more fully integrate Etruria into a world that stretched the length and readth of the Mediterranean Sea: a fact reflected in the rich contents of the cemeteries of Tarquinia to the north and Caere/Cerveteri to the south. Both of these cemeteries are now on the UNESCO World Heritage site list.

It was the Roman Emperor Trajan, however, who first realized the tremendous economic and strategic potential offered by enlarging the tiny, natural harbor. And to do so, in 106, he commissioned the internationally known Syrian architect, Apollo of Damascus, who had designed and built his magnificent forum in Rome.

The Greek wine god Dionysos (Bacchus to the Romans) sailing among dolphins is depicted on the inside of this drinking cup *(kylix)* made in Athens by the famous artist Exekias *c.* 530 BCE. It was subsequently exported to Etruria where it was found in a young man's tomb in Vulci.
Staatliche Antikensammlungen (Munich). Inv. 2044. Photo by Matthias Kabel (Wikimedia Commons, CC BY-SA 3.0)

In order to oversee construction, Trajan built a second home nearby, described as a "beautiful villa overlooking the sea" by his friend and advisor, Pliny the Younger (*Epistolae,* 6.31). Wealth attracted wealth, and soon other villas sprouted up, each displaying a high degree of cultural internationalism. At nearby Santa Marinella, ancient *Castrum Novum,* a five-foot marble statue of Athena has been discovered, a copy of the famous statue carved by Phidias in 438 BCE for her temple on the Athenian Acropolis. This was most probably made in a 2nd century workshop specializing in reproductions of Greek masterpieces for the local elites.

Pliny has also left us the oldest (surviving) reference to the name of the port as "Centumcellae," perhaps in reference to the 100 rooms (cells) of Trajan's magnificent villa. The name caught on and was carried well into Byzantine times. Sailing from Rome to Gaul in the year 416, the Roman poet Rutilius Namatianus put in here and described a very enjoyable day spent at the baths. That era was coming to an end, however, for this was one of the last spots on the Tyrrhenian coast that could provide a traveler with such amenities.

Centumcellae was incorporated into the Papal States *c.* 700 and, at first, the power of the Papacy was sufficient to protect the few who huddled around the remnants of the ancient port. But, in 828, the Saracens finally prevailed and chased the last inhabitants into the neighboring hills. There they would remain for generations before it was safe to return to their old city: to their *civita vecchia.*

In 1508, Pope Julius II ("The Warrior Pope") called on Bramante to design and build a fortress to protect the harbor, utilizing as its base a large structure that ıad once housed the rowers of the Roman imperial navy (tombstones ›f some can be seen in the Archaeological Museum, Largo Cavour, ?). It was massive in plan, with four turrets and an octagonal "keep" *donjon)*, but construction slowed upon Bramante's death and his vork lay unfinished—and useless—when the mutinous troops of Charles V passed through on their way to sack the Eternal City in .527. It would take another decade, and the genius of Michelangelo, o complete the task. Finally, in 1660, Bernini converted the ›ld Roman dockyard *(dassena)* into a landing for smaller ships ınd it is still used as such by the local fishermen of today.

A copy of the Athena Parthenos, found at Santa Marinella, illustrates the sophistication of the population in the 2nd century. Civitavecchia Archaeological Museum.
Photo courtesy of the Time Traveling Gourmet.

)espite the combined efforts of so much architectural talent, a lisgruntled D.H. Lawrence dismissed Civitavecchia in *Etruscan Places* as "a port of not much importance" after arriving by train luring the nascent *fascismo* days of Mussolini's ascendency. In he little port's defense, however, the railroad had only recently ırrived, malaria was still rampant, and WW II loomed darkly on he horizon. Given time, however, the sleepy little harbor would ›vercome these and other obstacles to eventually become *the* port ›f Rome. Today it handles the highest volume of passengers and he largest brute tonnage of cargo that passes to and from Rome, lown the A12, a Roman road (the Via Aurelia) that was already :enturies old when Emperor Trajan began work on the harbor.

Local Grape Varieties

With the exception of Frascati (ancient Roman Tusculum), Lazio has ıever enjoyed a reputation for great wines. However, with the awarding ›f *Denominazione di Origine Controllata* ("Controlled Designation ›f Origin") status for the wines of Cerveteri in 1974, followed by hose of Tarquinia in 1996, the area has really come into its own. In Civitavecchia the story of wine is essentially a tale of these two DOCs.

Nomenclature for the local wines is about to undergo another change vith the creation of a new IGP *(Indicazione Geographica Protetta)* that vill cover the entire coastal area from Civitavechia south to Fiumicino. t will be known as the Costa Etrusco Romano appellation and will allow he inclusion of two additional white grapes: **Fiano** (Fee-YA-no), possibly he Roman *vitis apiana,* to contribute a degree of honeyed richness; and **Vermentino** (Ver-men-TEEN-o), widely planted on Sardinia and Corsica, to ›rovide acidity, a degee of minerality, and its distinctive aroma/perfume.

WHITE GRAPES

Two grapes bearing the name Trebbiano serve as the backbone for the white wines n both DOCs, each delivering its own crisp acidity to the structure of the wine.

CERVETERI and TARQUINIA DOCs

WHITE (BIANCO)	RED (ROSSO)
Primary Grapes:	***Primary Grapes:***
Trebbiano Toscana *or*	Sangiovese *or*
Trebbiano Giallo	Montepulciano d'Abruzzo
Major Blending Grapes:	***Major Blending Grapes:***
Malvasia di Candia *or*	Cesanese *or*
Malvasia del Lazio	Abbuoto
Wine Types:	***Wine Types:***
Bianco Secco (dry)	Rosso Secco (dry)
Bianco Frizzante (slightly sparkling)	Novello Rosso (new)
Bianco Amabile (semi-sweet)	Rosso Dolce (sweet)

Trebbiano Toscana (Treb-YA-no tos-KA-na), known elsewhere as Ugni Blanc and St. Émilion, is a large-clustered grape that begs the adjective "ubiquitous," as it is one of the most widely planted grapes in the world. While its origin is debated, some associate the grape with an Etruscan town of similar name, while others believe it to be related to the *vinum trebulanum* mentioned by Pliny the Elder in his *Naturalis Historiae.* The second grape, **Trebbiano Giallo** (Treb-YA-no jee-YA-lo), has recently been shown by Massimo Labra and his colleagues at the University of Milan to be related to Toscana in name only.

The Trebbiano grape is elsewhere known as Ugni Blanc.
Photo by Pancrat (Wikimedia Commons, CC BY-SA 3.0).

The major white blending grapes, **Malvasia di Candia** (Mal-vah-SEE-ah dee Candi-yah) and **Malvasia del Lazio** (Mal-vah-SEE-ah del-LA-zyo), are also genetically distinct and therefore unrelated. They contribute a floral quality to both the nose and palette that helps to balance, and build on, the Trebbiano core. Other white varietals are permitted in small amounts but, for some reason, **Pinot Grigio** is explicitly excluded.

RED GRAPES

Two red grapes are paramount here. **Sangiovese** (San-jyo-VAY-zay), whose name may derive from the Latin *Sanguis Jovis* ("Blood of Jove/Jupiter"), and **Montepulciano d'Abruzzo** (Mon-te-pull-chee-ya-noh Da-BRUZ-zo), not to be confused with Tuscany's **Vino Nobile di Montepulciano**). The two are often combined in simple, 60/40 blends but other red grapes are permitted (up to 30%), including the contrary **Cesanese** (Chay-sa-NAY-zay) and the rarely used **Abbuoto** (A-boo-OH-to).

A Special Treat

isitors with a special interest in "wines ˈplace" must try those made from the **iacché** (Jya-KAY) grape produced by e Collacciani family at the Casale Cento orvi Winery on the outskirts of Cerveteri, escribed as *il vino nato prima di Roma.* hat's right! Wine born before the city of ome: an event traditionally assigned to e year 753 BC when much of the area was nder Etruscan control. Said to have been xcavated in one of the hundreds of Etruscan mbs in Cerveteri's Banditaccia Cemetery, eeds of the Giacché grape were grown out, afted onto modern rootstock, and are now ature vines that produce a pair of unique GP wines. Grapes for Giacché Rosso (AKA osso Lazio) are harvested relatively late in ctober and, after fermentation in stainless eel tanks and a secondary (malolactic) rmentation in (untoasted) American and ench oak, produce a big, robust wine.

Clusters of Sangiovese grapes from the Montalcino region of Tuscany.
Photo by O. Strama (Wikimedia Commons, CC BY-SA 3.0).

the Giacché Passito Lazio the grapes ave been partially desiccated in order to concentrate their juice, intensify eir flavor, and increase the sugar-to-water ratio that will result in a wine ith a higher alcohol level (15–16% ABV). Unlike other *passito* (Pah-SEE-to) ines, however, the grapes are not dried on mats. Instead, the bunches are lowed to hang on the vine for a month or more after being "strangled" (the t of *la strozzatura*, from *strozzare* – to strangle or choke). While the vine emains alive, these specially treated bunches develop sugar and deepen their oma/perfume until the mid-November harvest. Fermented in temperature-ontrolled, stainless steel tanks, the wine develops remarkable complexity ith dark red stone fruits and structured tannins prominent on the palate.

asale Cento Corvi also grows other "Italian" grapes such as Montepulciano, an Giovese, Malvasia, and Trebbiano, as well as several international varietals hardonnay, Merlot, etc.), thus producing a wide spectrum of wines. They e often bottled under labels that pay homage to the area's rich Etrusco-oman past. These include **Kantharos** (with reference to the large two-handled inking cup that was a favorite of Dionysos), and **Kottabos**, the drinking me played at both Etruscan and Greek *symposia* (drinking parties) that is ten depicted on tomb walls and the interior of drinking cups (*kylikes*).

Wine Bar

Many of these wines can be sampled in a spot that is popular with both locals and the author. It is conveniently located on the Via Cesare Battesi (opposite no. 15), marked only by the single word: *Enoteca* (in very faded signage). Pass through to a back room filled with dusty wine bottles and B&W photos of jazz musicians to choose from a wide selection of local wines by the glass, each served with an appropriate mezze. This is the perfect place to dally with that special someone.

The Etruscans' joy of life is palpable in the banquet scenes that decorate the walls of their tombs and, unlike the somewhat similar Greek symposium, their convivium included women as integral partners. The 5th century BCE Tomb of the Leopards, Tarquinia. Photo by AlMare (Wikimedia Commons, PD)

Sweet Tooth

Lazio is famous for its *maritozzi con la panna,* sweet brioche-style buns filled with freshly whipped cream, and Civitavecchia is no exception. Try the ones at *Chalet del Pincio*, close to the port at Via Michelangelo Buonarroti 3 (just off the Via Francesco Crispi). The line of customers can be long, but the maritozzi are well worth the wait, and the same can be said for their all-natural gelato.

Known as the Capitoline Wolf *(Lupa Capitolina)*, this bronze sculpture was once thought to have been crafted by a 5th century BCE Etruscan artist, but it is now considered to have been made in the 11th–12th century. The figures of young Romulus and Remus were added during the Renaissance Period (15th century).
Capitoline Museum, Palazzo dei Conservatori (Wikimedia Commons, PD).

Cheers!

In Civitavecchia,
just say

Cin Cin!

(chin-chin)

Note: The author wishes to thank Benedetto Zapicchi, who excavated the Banditaccia Cemetery in the 1970's, for taking the time to discuss the excavations. He is the author of *Cerveteri: Le Necropoli della Banditaccia e altri monumenti ceriti* (published by *La Fondazione Archeologica per l'Etruria Meridionale*, Santa Marinella, 2006).

Dubrovnik

Croatia

Praised as the Pearl of the Adriatic by Irish Playwright George Bernard Shaw, Dubrovnik is nestled behind walls that were built as early as the 12th century. They continued to protected the city while it functioned as the core of the Republic of Ragusa (1358–1808), and today serve as a distinctive icon of the city.
Photo by Martin Falbisoner (Wikimedia Commons, CC BY-SA 4.0).

As a country, Croatia is both very old and very new. Archaeologists have traced human habitation there all the way back to the Stone Age, and it had formed part of the Roman Province of Pannonia for centuries before the Slavic "Croats" arrived in the 7th century. Dubrovnik prospered as the capital of the Republic of Ragusa (1358–1808), a very enlightened republic, whose merchant ships sailed under a white flag bearing the single word "*Libertas*" after abolishing the slave trade in 1418. But, as a modern entity, Croatia is less than three decades old. In 1991, at the breakup of Yugoslavia, it declared itself to be an independent, democratic, parliamentary republic and was recognized as such by the United Nations the following year.

St. Blaise, a Fourth century martyr, was the patron saint of Dubrovnik. He appears frequently, with his hand raised in benediction, on the coinage of the Republic of Ragusa.
Photo courtesy of CNG (Auction 410, Lot 469).

Geographically, Croatia consists of a long and narrow stretch of land along the rocky Adriatic Coast that is separated by low mountains from the fertile Pannonian Plain that reaches inland past Zagreb and southward to the banks of the Danube River. The history of wine growing in this area goes back at least as far as the 5th century BCE, when Greeks began trading with the myriad of small islands that are scattered along the Dalmatian Coast.

Legendary winemaker Miljenko ("Mike") Grgich, the man who put California on the wine-world's map when his Chardonnay won the famous Judgment of Paris in 1976.
Photo by Adrian Gregorutti, courtesy of Grgich Hills Estate.

This close juxtaposition of both Mediterranean and Continental microclimates contributes to the wide range of grape varietals and wine types that are available in the country today. It also divides the country into two distinct wine growing regions (Coastal and Continental), each with about a half-dozen sub-regions. It follows, then, that the names of Croatian wines would emphasize their geographic origin rather than the specific grape(s) from which they are made. Recently, the Croatian Institute of Viticulture and Enology has introduced a Protected Geographical Origin (PGO) system, similar to that used elsewhere in Europe, that is beginning to clarify and simplify the situation.

Without a doubt the most widely recognized name in Croatian winemaking is Miljenko ("Mike") Grgich. It was Mike who crafted the famous 1973 Chateau Montelena Alexander Valley Chardonnay that beat all comers (in a blind tasting) at the legendary "Judgement of Paris" in 1976!

With this success and many others under his belt, Mike came home to Croatia and in 1996 built a state-of-the art winery near the port of Trstenik, in the central part of the Pelješac Peninsula, not far from Dubrovnik. It incorporates many of the techniques that he had used in crafting his Napa Valley wines at Grgich Hills Estates in Rutherford, CA. His wines from the regions of Dingać and Postup (see below) are some of the best on the market.

Dubrovnik is situated at the extreme southern end of a long coastal strip, hard against the borders of Bosnia & Herzegovina and Montenegro. Here more than 200 indigenous grape varietals, both red (*Crno* = TSIRno, literally "black") and white (*Bijelo* = B'YELL-low), have been identified. Below are a few of the wines made from those grapes. Most of them will be encountered easily during a brief visit to this historic port.

Local Grape Varietals

WHITE GRAPES

Pošip (POE-ship) is an indigenous Croatian white grape that for centuries has been a main focus of winemakers on the island of Korcula, located just off the western coast of the Pelješac Peninsula. This is the island that many historians believe to have been the birthplace of Marco Polo.

'hen this grape is grown on steep, sunny slopes it produces a ;ht and refreshing wine with a citrus (grapefruit) edge and a ish that is often described as "bitter almond." The Marco Polo and of Pošip, made on the island by the Agricultural Cooperative Cara, is a very good, popular, and readily available example of ıat the grape can do.

ıe **Vugava** (Voo-GAV-ah) grape, closely related to Viognier, oduces a higher alcohol white wine (often 14% plus) whose :k of acidity can often make it seem stale and flabby. A popular ne from this grape is made on the Dalmatian island of Vis, the cient Greek colony of Issa. In antiquity, wine from this island ıs celebrated as far away as the Nile Valley, where a famous urmand (Athenaeus of Naukratis) boasted that the wine om Issa was "better than any other" (*Deipnosophistae* I.28d). ıfortunately, wine made on the island today does not seem to ırrant the same elevated status, but it is still worth a taste.

:k (Gerk), another indigenous Croatian white grape, produces lry, aromatic wine. It is a very old and primitive grape whose ıes produce only female flowers, and so it must be pollinated male vines (often Plavac Mali) that are purposely planted arby. Today Grk is grown commercially in a very limited area, d the wines made from the grape are difficult to find. But : search—if you are successful—is well worth the effort.

ED GRAPES

avac Mali (PLAAH-vaahts MOLL-ly), the most famous the Croatian red wine grapes, produces a dry, full died wine with substantial structure and character.

the past, Plavac Mali has been thought to be entical with either the Italian Primitivo or the ıerican Zinfandel grape. Recent attempts to define : grape's parentage, through DNA profiling, seem times to solve, and at other times to confound, : situation. The conversation continues.

ıe finest examples of Plavac Mali's potential iginate in the vineyards of Dingač and Postup on the ınny Pelješac (PELL-yay-shots) Peninsula north of ıbrovnik, and from acreage on the island of Hvar.

:nerally these full-bodied wines exhibit aromas stone fruit, almonds, and even sage and, while uthful wines may show aggressive tannins, ıs usually mellows with a little bottle age.

The statue of the young knight Orlando (Roland) standing in Luza Square with his back turned toward St. Blaise Cathedral is steeped in medieval history. For more than six centuries it has served to symbolize Dubrovnik's independence and, at one time, the length of his right forearm (51.25 cm) even functioned as the standard of measurement for the city's fabric merchants. To celebrate this anniversary, the year 2019 was proclaimed as the "Year of Orlando."
Photo by Bizutage (Wikimedia Commons, CC BY-SA 3.0).

The main street of Dubrovnik's Old Town began life as a swampy channel separating the island of Ragusa from the wooded settlement of Dubrovnik, before it was filled toward the end of the end of the 13th century. Also known as Placa, this 300 m pedestrian avenue forms the heart of the modern town.
Photo by László Szalai, Beyond Silence (Wikimedia Commons, CC BY-SA 3.0).

Dingać (DING-gotch) is a tiny section of the Pelješac Peninsula with steep slopes facing the sea where the vines are warmed by a combination of direct sunshine and light reflected off the water. This microclimate is considered to be so distinctive that for year the integrity of its terroir has been protected by the International Geneva Convention.

Plavac Mali wines grown in Dingać will often show a slightly "sweet" edge to an otherwise dry and full-bodied wine.

Postup (POST-oop), the area adjacent to the Dingać vineyards, is the second most important Plavac Mali growing area on the peninsula and one that is also registered for government protection (PGI). Superb Plavac Mali wines are produced here.

Hvar Island, often referred to as "Europe's sunniest island," provides the same combination of direct and reflected sunlight especially on the steep slopes above its southern coast. Grapes grown here produce well-structured wines similar to, but fruitier and less-alcoholic, than those made on the peninsula.

A Regional Specialty

After Roman Emperor Diocletian abdicated the throne he retired to his palace at Split, just to the north of Dubrovnik, where he is said to have passed his retirement years raising cabbages and drinking the sweet wines of his homeland.
Photo courtesy of CNG (Triton XIV, Lot 812).

Croatian Prošek is a wine that is often mis-translated as Prosecco and, consequently, confused with the light and sparkling wines of the Venetian hinterland. Dalmatian Prošek (PRO-shek), however, is a desert wine that is traditionally made from dried grapes, although some winemakers are now substituting cooked-down must for the sugar-rich raisins.

Prošek quickly became a favorite of the Roman Emperor Diocletian after he took up permanent residence in his palace at Split (ancient *Spalatum*) further up the Dalmatian Coast in the year 305.

Prošek can exhibit tremendous variety since much of it is homemade and each winemaker is free to select the grape varietals used. These are usually white grapes, but Zlatan Otok Winery on the Island of Hvar crafts a Prošek from the Plavac Mali grape. Also interesting is an oak-aged Prošek from

In the 9th century Dubrovnik was forced to endure a 15-month siege by Saracen corsairs before it was broken by the forces of Byzantine Emperor Basil I.
Photo: *Synopsis of Histories* by John Skylitzes, Biblioteca Nacional de España, Madrid (Wikimedia Commons, PD).

Hvar crafted from three of their local grapes: **Bogdanusa** (white), **Parć** (white), and **Trbljan** (red). Another tasty version, also made on Hvar, bears the name of Petar Hektorovic (1487–1572), a tribute to a famous Croatian poet who wrote extensively in the local dialect of the island rather than in the more customary Latin of his day. A prominent figure in the Croatian Literary Renaissance of the 15th–16th century, his boyhood home now houses the Ethnographic Museum.

Sweet as honey, Prošek is delicious—but be cautious: the alcohol can average 16%–17%.

Many historians believe that the famous traveler Marco Polo (1254–1324) was born not in Venice itself, but in the town of Korcula on the Croatian island of the same name. Here he appears dressed as a wealthy Tartar merchant.

Grevembrock, *Coureurs des mers*. Poivre d'Arvor (Wikimedia Commons, PD).

Celebrate!

If your stop in Dubrovnik calls for a celebration, keep an eye out for "a bottle of bubbly" from Misal, the largest Croatian producer of sparkling wines.

Located in Istria, at the northern end of the Dalmatian coast, the Misal Winery offers a dozen or so sparkling wines in a variety of styles and colors (Brut, Sec, Demi-Sec, etc.). Using classic Pinot Noir (known locally as **Pinot Crni**) and/or Chardonnay grapes, they will often substitute a local grape such as **Istrian Malmsey** for the traditional Pinot Meunier. One of their most interesting sparklers, Misal Noir, uses the juice of the indigenous Istrian **Borgonja** grape as its base wine and then blends in small percentages of two other local red grapes, **Hrvatica** (the Italian **Croatina**) and **Teran** (the Italian **Terrano**), to achieve its distinctive (black coffee) color and delightful taste.

Wine Bars

D'Vino Wine Bar (located in the *Stari Grad* at Palmoticeva Street 4a, just three streets in from the Pile Gate) boasts the largest and most diverse selection of wines by the glass in Dubrovnik, offering over 100 domestic and international wines from which to choose.

This is a small, cozy place whose wide selection of quality wines is surpassed only by the expertise and enthusiasm of their young staff.

Sure, they will serve you a glass of wine, or sell you a bottle to bring back to the ship, but they will also take the time to teach you which wine to buy, and why you should buy it. Sit down and enjoy one of their pre-planned flights, designed to illustrate a specific varietal or terroir, or they will create a tasting especially for you. Whether you come alone or in a group, the staff at D'Vino simply wants to teach you about their favorite subject: the wines of Croatia.

Wine Words to Watch For

Croatian wine labels often contain these hints as to the style and quality of the wine inside:

Kvalitetno – Quality

Polusuho – Semi-dry

Rosa – Rosé

Slatk – Sweet

Stolno Vino – Table Wine

Suho – Dry

Vrhunsko – Premium

The larger of two fountains constructed by Onofrio della Cava *c.*1440 carried water by gravity-feed over seven miles to the plaza in front of St. Savior's Church in Dubrovnik. It was originally topped by a cupola built by Milanese architect Petar Martinov that was destroyed in the earthquake of 1667.
Photo by Neoneo13 (Wikimedia Commons, PD).

Bottle Shops

The *D'Vino Wine Bar* will send you off with bottles of your favorite wines, but if your time is limited and your shopping list includes more than just wine (such as gifts for friends and family back home) check out *Dubrovacka Kuca*, located on Svetog Dominika *(Stari Grad)*. In addition to a large selection of Croatian artwork and embroidery, they also offer a wide spectrum of regional agricultural products such as honey, olive oil, and a very good selection of local Dalmatian wines and *rakija* (high alcohol "brandies" made from a variety of local fruits).

At a meal in Dubrovnik, wine is often diluted with still water and called *gemišt*, or with sparkling water and called *bevanda*. Enjoy!

Beer (Pivo)

Croatia has several breweries but the two largest, and most readily accessible, are Karlovako Pivo, founded in 1854, and Ožujsko Pivo, founded in 1893. Their offerings are widely available in bottles, cans, and on tap.

A special "Thank You" is due to Ms Violet Grgich for assisting the author with the pronunciation of several of the Croatian words used here. Any errors are, of course, his own.

For further reading: M. Horkey and C. Tan, *Cracking Croatian Wine: A Visitor Friendly Guide*. Exotic Wine Travel, 2017.

Heraklion/Iraklion

Crete, Greece

ne port of Heraklion/Iraklion is still guarded by the little *Kulesi*, a fortress built by the Venetians in the 16th century.
oto by Bernard Gagnon (Wikimedia Commons, CC BY-SA 3.0).

It is said that Crete was once the home of King Minos—son of Zeus and Europa—who ruled from a splendid palace at the site of Knossos protected, not by walls of stone, but by the strength of his powerful navy. lthough praised for his wisdom and fairness, Herodotus tells us that Minos 'as vilified for demanding that King Aegeus of Athens send him an annual etachment of young Athenians to be devoured by a terrifying creature ıat was half-man and half-bull. This bloodthirsty "Minotaur" roamed the orridors of a labyrinth (maze) built at Knossos by the legendary craftsman aedalus. That is, until a young Athenian named Theseus, abetted by Minos' omely daughter Ariadne, entered the labyrinth and killed the monster.

An early 4th century BCE silver *drachma* from Knossos, depicting the maze that housed the fearsome Minotaur, reinforces the tradition that this was considered to have been the home of the legendary King Minos.
Photo courtesy of the Classical Numismatic Group, Inc. (http://www.cngcoins.com).

t the end of the 19th century, on a low hill south of the modern port of eraklion, traces of architecture, bits of pottery, and coins struck with ıe word "Knossos" began to be noticed. Subsequent excavation there evealed a very impressive, un-walled building that was identified as a alace and almost immediately attributed to the legendary King Minos.

The gentler side of the young Minotaur's personality is shown as he sits on his mother's lap. Detail from a drinking cup (*kylix*) painted by the Settecamini Painter in Athens, *c.* 340–320 BCE. From Vulci.
Bibliothèque nationale de France, Cabinet des Médailles (Wikimedia Commons, PD)

Unfortunately, toward the end of the 2nd Millennium BCE, Minos' navy failed him, and his magnificent palace—the symbol of the once-proud Minoan state—was destroyed by agents uncertain. Life around Knossos would continue to sputter along for centuries, characterized by constant internecine squabbles with neighboring city-states such as Gortyn, Kydonia, and Lyttos. Rarely, however, was one of them powerful enough to prevent the island from becoming a haven for pirates. For that task a strong central government would be required and Rome, waiting in the wings, was only too willing to oblige.

After a long siege, Quintus Caecilius Metellus and three legions conquered the island in 69 BCE and brought it into the Roman sphere. Although Gortyn became the seat of the new Roman governor, Knossos would enjoy a high level of prosperity to which the rich mosaics in the Villa Dionysus (2nd century) bear powerful witness. It was around this time that references to a Cretan port named *Heracleum* began to appear in the literature.

With the break-up of the Roman Empire in the 4th century, Christian Crete aligned itself with the Byzantine East and would remain so until 824 when the island was captured by Abu Hafs and a group of Saracen Arab refugees (*sarkenoi*) from Spanish Andalusia. The port of Heracleum became part of the Emirate of Crete and its name was changed to *Rabdh el-Khandak* ("The Fortress of the Moat"). It would be almost two centuries before Byzantine armies under Nikephoros Phokas were able to dislodge the Muslims and restore the island's ties with Constantinople, and with Christianity.

In the aftermath of the Fourth Crusade and the fall of Constantinople in 1204, the island of Crete was awarded to Boniface de Monferrato who quickly handed it off to the Doge of Venice, for a thousand pieces of silver. The Khandak of the Saracens now became the *Chandax/Candia* of the Venetians, who surrounded the town with massive walls, some estimated to be over 40 feet thick! They also "modernized" its harbor defenses by adding the little fortress known today as *Kulesi*.

A bust of the young wine-god, on display in the Heraklion Museum, may have originally stood in the 2nd century Roman Villa of Dionysus at Knossos.
Photo by Zdeněk Kratochvíl (Wikimedia Commons, CC BY-SA 4.

Sadly, Crete continued to attract more than its share of pirates (including the notorious Barbarosa) and it soon caught the eye of the expanding Ottoman Empire. The Siege of Candia, again pitting Muslim against Christian, began in 1648. Crete was able to hold out for more than two decades but, despite assistance sent by Louis XIV and Pope Clement IX, Candia fell. Its citizenry was dispersed. Neglect and indifference settled in. The island became a backwater rife with religious and ethnic strife. Below the surface, Cretan resentment for its Ottoman rulers seethed.

A 3500 year old wine press from the large Minoan building at Vathypetro, just to the south of Heraklion.

Photo by Schuppi (Wikimedia Commons, CC BY-SA 3.0).

Finally, in the 19th century, after the Great Powers of Europe had interjected their collective ignorance into the mix, Crete rose up in open revolt under the banner of "Freedom or Death." Through the sacrifices of mustachioed patriots in highland villages and the work of astute diplomats, Zorba's island achieved its freedom in 1898. Union with Greece followed in 1913. And, in spite of Nazi occupation (1941–1945) and rule by a military junta (1969–1974), it remains so today—with Heraklion (Iraklion) as its capital.

Local Grape Varieties

While Heraklion has never been a stranger to those who practiced the winemaker's craft, the modern history of Cretan wine began in the 1950s when the Miliarakis brothers (local suppliers and bulk exporters) had the novel idea of selling their wines in glass bottles, complete with paper labels identifying their MiNOS brand (now also Minoïko and Minos Palace). In the following decades they were joined by the Peza Agricultural Union Cooperative, the Lyrarakis Winery and, recently, the Boutari Winery (Fantaxométoho Estate) to form the backbone of the modern Cretan winemaking industry. To these larger enterprises, several smaller—excellent—wineries must be added (see below), all of which are connected by the well-organized Wine Roads of Crete program.

Whether their operation is large or small, the winemakers of Crete possess a passion for the identification, protection, and vinification of the grape varieties that are indigenous, or historically important, to their island. **Plyto** (Plee-TO) and **Daphni** (Daf-NEE) were brought back from near extinction by Manolis Lyrarakis whose family winery now offers a PGI wine of each, and **Muscat Spiná** (Mus-kat Spee-NA), a rare, thin-skinned variety of the Muscat grape was rescued through the efforts of Yanis Konstantakakis of Boutari's Domaine Fantaxométoho facility where a PGI wine is crafted from it today.

WHITE GRAPES

The **Vilana** (Vil-LA-na) grape is the "rock star" of Cretan white wine production. If you order white wine in Heraklion it will almost certainly contain a percentage of Vilana, while single varietal PDO and PGI Vilana wines are produced by almost every Cretan winemaker. This pale yellow cultivar produces fresh, fruity, and aromatic wines in a wide variety of styles. Their green apple crispness, combined with a relatively low level of alcohol (*c.* 11.8 %), make them especially food-friendly and best when consumed young. Miliarakis, the first to age its white wines in oak, features a Vilana Fume that bends the flavor curve toward apricot/peach while picking up a layer of vanilla from the time spent in the barrel. Vilana is successfully blended with other local varieties such as **Thrapsathiri** (Thrap-sa-THI-ri), **Ladikinon** (Lad-ik-i-NON), and/or **Vidiano** (Vid-i-a-NO).

The Vilana grape.

Photo from *The Cretan Grapes*, by Maritina Stavrakaki and Manolis N. Stavrakakis, Tropi Publications, Athens. With the kind permission of the authors.

RED GRAPES

Red wines emphasize three local grape varieties.

Mandilari(a) (Man-di-LAR-i-ya) is indigenous to Crete and grows particularly well in the Peza and Arkhanes appellations where its late-ripening fruit produces PGI wines of a deep, ruby color. These wines exhibit dark stone fruit aromas with acceptable tannins but are often quite low in alcohol. Lyrarakis offers an interesting 100% Mandilaria wine from its low-yield "Plakoura" vineyard that is aged in French and American oak (12.5% ABV), as well as a Mandilari Rosé: fresh and fruity (think ripe raspberries). This is a perfect wine for a summer afternoon.

The Kotsifali grape.

Photo from *The Cretan Grapes*, by Maritina Stavrakaki and Manolis N. Stavrakakis, Tropi Publications, Athens. With the kind permission of the authors.

Kotsifali (Kot-si-FAH-li), the second red grape, is also associated with Peza & Archanes. A low-acid grape with a deficiency of anthocyanins, it yields weak red wines (often with an orange tinge), but its naturally high sugar offers higher alcohol and greater aging potential. Varietal Kotsifali red wines are the exception (although Lyrarakis makes two, and Miliarakis even makes a white wine from it!), and it is usually blended with Mandilari. Because one grape's weakness is the other grape's strength they work well together and form the backbone of the Cretan red wine blends. 75% Kotsifali to 25% Mandilari is the starting point for many of the Peza/Arkhanes reds. Vinification methods vary considerably and some may even include a little time in oak. A good introduction is Boutari's **Kretikos** red—available in most restaurants.

Liatiko (Lee-YA-ti-ko) is a vigorous, early-ripening grape that produces its clusters of small, oval, brown-skinned berries

The European Union's Regulations on Wine as an Agricultural Product (EU #607/2009).

WINE CATEGORY	DESCRIPTION/REQUIREMENT
PDO Wines *"Protected Designation of Origin"*	Previously categorized by appellation of origin (VQPRD, OPAP, AOC, etc.).
PGI Wines *"Protected Geographical Indication"* with a specific geographical provenance.	All "Regional Wines" and "Traditional Wines"
Varietal Wines	May indicate the year of vintage and the varietal composition, but not the specific geographic origin.
Table Wines	*Vin ordinaire.* May include other information, but without indication of either the vintage or varietal(s).

mid-summer, as its name (an abbreviation of *Iouliatiko,* meaning "of ly") would imply. When fermented dry, Liatiko makes a high alcohol, low id wine with soft tannins that drinks better with some age. Especially ell made is Douloufakis' single varietal, PDO **Daphnios** from vineyards the village of Daphnes. Its aromatics and fruity flavors led the 2012 ntage to be described as "pretty sexy" in the *Wine Advocate* (12/20/12). n the sweet side, both Douloufakis' **Helios** and Boutari's **Iouliatiko** dry eir grapes for about ten days in the sun and finish their wine in oak efore bottling in 500 ml bottles. Many believe that Liatiko as the grape used to make Malvasia, the sweet wine that has ought fame to the island since the 15th century (see below).

Special Treat

iporo (TSEE-po-ro) is a strong, grappa-like liquor widely njoyed throughout Greece. On Crete, it is known as *Tsikoudia* see-koo-THYAH), a name whose specific geographic etermination is guaranteed by the EU. Around Heraklion, is clear (deceptively innocent) distillate is known colloquially *Raki* (Ra-KEE), not to be confused with Turkish *rakı* that is milar to Greek *ouzo* in that both are processed with aniseed using them to turn milky when water or ice is added.

raditionally, raki has been made in small batches by families at e end of the grape harvest by fermenting, and then distilling, e residual must, seeds, stems, and skins. However, a few ommercial producers such as the Kallikratis Distillery do exist nd they facilitate the sharing of this local specialty with others.

The iconic MiNOS label from the first Cretan wine to be sold in bottles (1952). Its iconography is proudly based on wall paintings in the so-called Palace of Minos.

Photo courtesy of Nicolas Miliarakis.

Variations on the theme include *Meloraki* (Meh-loh-RA-ki) that incorporates Cretan honey (*mele*) to temper the fire, and *Mournoraki* (Moor-no-RA-ki), a red variant distilled from the fruit of the mulberry tree (*mouro*).

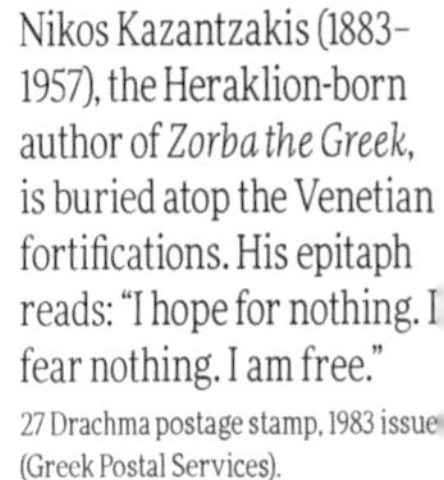

Nikos Kazantzakis (1883–1957), the Heraklion-born author of *Zorba the Greek*, is buried atop the Venetian fortifications. His epitaph reads: "I hope for nothing. I fear nothing. I am free."

27 Drachma postage stamp, 1983 issue (Greek Postal Services).

Celebrate!

A great way to celebrate a special occasion in Heraklion would be with a glass of *Malvasia/Malvazia* (Mal-va-S/ZI-a) *di Candia*, the sweet, raisined wine that, during the Venetian occupation (14th–16th centuries), became legendary throughout the Mediterranean world. However, since few can agree on how it was made, and from which grape(s), we are left with a situation that even recent DNA studies find difficult to resolve. Because modern versions vary, why not celebrate with a selection? Be sure to include Douloufakis' **Malvasia di Candia Aromatico**, a straight-forward single varietal and Lyrarakis' **Malvasia of Crete**, a more complex blend of four sundried local grapes (Plyto, Daphní, Vilana, and Vidiana).

Musician Nikos Xilouris (1936–1980), "The Archangel of Crete," often wore the headdress (*sariki*) of the mountain men who fought for Cretan independence from Turkish tyranny. His voice defied the military junta and it is still heard today—whenever, and wherever, injustice is perceived. The Nikos Xilouris Museum is in the village of Anoigia, Crete.

Bottle Shops & Tasting Rooms

Its name, *Cash n'Carry – ZOGRAPHAKI*, might sound like a convenience store, but it is a genuine purveyor of wines and spirits and, at Korai St. 17, is only a short walk from the Archaeological Museum. Slightly further afield, at Papandréou Georgíou St. 19, *Kava Néktal* is reached by a pleasant walk along the Venetian fortifications. If you do not have the time to visit the tasting rooms in the hinterland, do not miss *Ktima Strataridakis* (KTEE-ma Strat-ar-i-DAK-is) on Kornaros Square (no. 46), named after the author of the *Erotokritos*, a 10,000-verse poem composed in the Cretan dialect during the early 17th century. Their knowledgeable staff pours, and discusses, wines crafted in what is said to be the southernmost winery in Europe.

Cheers!

In Heraklion,
just say

YIA-mas!

("To/For Us")

Istanbul

Turkey

Hagia Sophia has looked down upon the Bosphorus for almost 1500 years. Begun as a church in the year 537, it served as such until 1453 when it was converted into a mosque. Secularized by Atatürk in 1935, Hagia Sophia now serves the world as a museum.
Photo by Arild Vågen (Wikimedia Commons, CC BY-SA 3.0).

East meets West in Istanbul, and myth meets history here as well. Europe and Asia are separated only by the turgid waters of the Hellespont, the narrow waterway also known as the Bosphorus in reference to Zeus' love affair with a beautiful mortal named Io. In order to hide her from the wrath of his jealous wife, Hera, Zeus turned his paramour into a heifer who wandered off across the Hellespont thus providing its alternate name. Bosphorus means "cow ford" in Greek. Later, when Io regained her human form, she gave birth to a daughter who subsequently bore a son named Byzas. In 667 BCE, he sailed into the estuary now known as the Golden Horn (*chrysokeras*) and established a colony that would bear his name for over a thousand years: Byzantion, later Latinized as Byzantium.

Byzas, the legendary founder of Byzantium, as depicted on a coin from the 2nd–3rd century.
Photo by World Imaging (Wikimedia Commons, CC BY-SA 3.0).

Although its strategic location made it prey to the many armies that crossed the Hellespont during the pre-Christian centuries, Byzantium flourished and eventually conquered its "sister city" of Chalcedon (modern Kadıköy) on the Asian side of the strait. In 73 BCE it was incorporated into the Roman Empire, the same year that a Thracian

The famous horses (quadriga) of Saint Mark's Basilica in Venice, which once graced the hippodrome in Constantinople, were but a small fraction of the loot that was sent back to Europe by the members of the Fourth Crusade in 1204.
Photo by Zairon (Wikimedia Commons, CC BY-SA 4.0).

gladiator named Spartacus began the slave revolt that would consume so much of Rome's military attention.

At first Rome treated Byzantium well, but when its people supported Pescennius Niger against Septimius Severus for the imperial crown, the latter attacked and by the year 195 he had starved the city into submission. He soon relented, however, and rebuilt the city, enlarging its defenses and adding a hippodrome large enough for crowds of 100,000 to watch as many as eight four-horse chariots competed in a single event. The hippodrome quickly became the focus of the city's social and political life and as *Sultan Ahmet Square* it remains a popular promenade today.

In the year 333, Constantine the Great made the city the capital of the predominantly Greek-speaking eastern half of the divided Roman Empire. Before cheering crowds he rededicated the city as the *Nova Roma* ("New Rome"), although in the popular parlance it would be known simply as Constantinople, The City *(polis)* of Constantine.

FIFTEEN CENTS
TIME
The Weekly News-Magazine
VOL. I, NO. 4
MUSTAPHA KEMAL PASHA
MARCH 24, 1923

Mustafa Kemal Atatürk, the founder of the modern Turkish state, appeared on the cover of TIME Magazine on March 24, 1923 (Vol. I, No. 4), only the fourth week of the magazine's existence
Artist: Gordon Stevenson (1892–1982), TIME Magazine (Wikimedia Commons, PD).

Shortly after his deathbed baptism Constantine ordered his son, Constantius II, to build a church upon the ruins of a pagan temple on the heights above the Bosphorus. Dedicated to the Divine Wisdom (*Hagia Sophia* in Greek) of his new god, the building would be destroyed twice during urban riots before Emperor Justinian rebuilt it on a grand scale in 537. In spite of a major insurrection that nearly cost him his life (the Nika Revolt) and a plague that killed about half of the population of his city, Justinian was able to marshal over 10,000 craftsmen and create the architectural masterpiece that has looked down on almost fifteen hundred years of the city's history.

And what history it has seen! Hostile advances by Persians, Avars, Slavs, Arabs, Bulgars, and Seljuk Turks were all turned back but, when the Latin Christians of the Fourth Crusade came calling, the handwriting was definitely on the wall. In April 1204, defenses that had protected the city for centuries were breached and three days of murder, rape, and looting ensued. The treasures of Constantinople were either sent off to the west or melted down on the spot.

ventually, the Latins were ousted but Byzantium ıd begun a slow and steady decline. Control ' its territory on both sides of the Bosphorus ›ntinued to shrink under the pressure of Osman hazi (1259–1326) and his "Ottoman" Turks as they ıme westward out of Central Anatolia, always ith their eye on the prize: Constantinople.

The Entry of Sultan Mehmet II into Constantinople on the 29th of May, 1453. Oil on canvas by Jean-Joseph Benjamin-Constant, *c.*1876.
Musée des Augustins, Toulouse, France (Wikimedia Commons, PD).

ıe flashpoint came in 1453, when young Sultan 'ehmet II ("the Conqueror"), a brilliant military ctician, set siege to the city in earnest and slowly began tighten the noose. Never intended to withstand the ınishment of gunpowder, the walls built by Theodosius in the 4th century simply crumbled. After a siege of ss than two months, the city capitulated. As the fighting ıbsided and the flames ebbed, Mehmet rode his stallion ght into Hagia Sophia and proclaimed that Justinian's agnificent basilica was now a mosque. Slowly, the ty began to take on a new face, an Islamic face, and ith this change came a new name. Substituting e Arabic suffix *-iyye* ("place") for the Greek *polis* city"), Constantinopolis became Konstantiniyye—but ost folk simply went on using a corruption of the reek phrase "to the city" (*is stin p/bolis*) or, as we would say today, Istanbul.

ıe last remnant of the mighty Roman Empire had ceased to exist. The Ottoman npire had taken its place. And for the next four centuries it would be ruled from ›pkapı Palace. There, beneath its High Gate, a succession of Sultans would greet gnitaries from around the world. Eventually this *Sublime Porte* became synonymous r both the Ottoman court and its government, and would remain so until the gning of the Treaty of Lausanne when the Sultanate was abolished and the modern ırkish state was born. On October 29, 1923, The Republic of Turkey was founded by ustafa Kemal Atatürk (1881–1938), and its capital was moved east to Ankara. Slowly tanbul took on a new life, a life of its own, the vibrant life that we experience today.

.ocal Grape Varieties

'ine had played an integral part in the lives of those who worshipped ionysus and Bacchus, and it was essential to the Christian liturgy. It was ss acceptable in Islam, however, and during the Moslem Sultanate most of e grape production was enjoyed as table grapes. Wine consumption did ve on among the minority Christian and Jewish communities and it made a ›meback after Atatürk, in his attempts to emphasize the secular state of the ew nation, helped establish its first commercial winery (Doluca) in the 1920s.

BUZBAĞ

A thirsty oenophile might be shocked when first confronted by a label with this word in large letters, but Kayra's Buzbağ (pronounced buuz-BAH) is actually a very popular wine brand in Turkey. Their wines compare well with these other high quality labels (listed alphabetically).

Doluca (founded 1926)
Kavaklıdere (founded 1929)
Kayra/Kaira (founded 1942)
Sevilen (founded 1942)
Turasan (founded 1943)
Vinkara (founded 2008)

At present, Turkey lacks a classification or appellation system so there are no regulations that would require a winemaker to use a minimum percentage of a certain grape variety in order to call the wine by that name. Attempts to create a geographic labeling system for the Kalecik Karası grape (see below) never gained much traction. And note that the paper strip (*banderole*) over the cork in a bottle of Turkish wine is not an indication of quality. It merely shows that all required taxes have been paid.

Local Grape Varietals

WHITE GRAPES

Narince (Nar-IN-djeh), meaning "delicate" in Turkish, is a grape with large, yellow-green berries that often exhibit considerable bronze discoloration. Indigenous to Tokat and the area to the southwest, it is one of the few grapes that can tolerate the cold climates of Cappadocia. Monocépage wines, such as Kavaklıdere's **Prestige Ancyra**, are pale yellow and light-bodied with a wide range of citrus flavors and a slightly mineral finish. Narince is very versatile. It blends well with other white varieties such as Emir (see below) and/or Semillon, and Kavaklıdere Winery has shown the grape's potential when allowed to mature in oak. They also use this grape to produce a fortified wine along the lines of a port (**Tatlı Sert White**).

Narince, a white grape indigenous to Tokat and Central Anatolia.
Vinkara Wines Inc., through the courtesy of Donna White.

Emir (Em-EER), Turkish for "ruler" or "commander," produces conical clusters of pale, greenish-yellow berries that also thrive in the cold climate and volcanic soils of Cappadocia. These grapes produce clean, crisp, high acid wines with green apple, citrus, and minerals on both the nose and palate. Single varietal Emir is best enjoyed when fresh (two year maximum). Emir blends well with Narince and oak maturation adds aging potential. Kavaklıdere's **Selection** series, Kayra's **Buzbağ** label, and Vinkara are all good examples.

RED GRAPES

Kalecik Karası (Kal-e-chek KA-RA-seh), a thick-skinned grape with a bluish tinge, is considered by many to be Turkey's finest wine grape. Boasting a pedigree as old as the Bronze Age Hittites, this grape was saved from near extinction by the tireless work of the University of Ankara's Faculty of Agriculture after phyloxera devastated the area in the 1960s. Indigenous to the Kalecik district in Central

Anatolia, it grows well along the Kızıl River (*Kızılırmak*) known to the ancient Greeks as the Halys River. Ruby in color and redolent of red stone fruit and an occasional hint of chocolate, these wines remind many of a fruity Pinot Noir or Gamay. Vinkara puts a very good Kalecik Karası in their smaller, 25 cl bottles (with clear, informative labels), that are often found in Turkish hotel minibars.

Kalecik Karası, an indigenous red grape from the Kalecik district in Central Anatolia.
Vinkara Wines Inc., through the courtesy of Donna White.

Although the **Boğazkere** (BOY-AZ-keh-reh) grape is indigenous to Elazığ (el-a-ZI) Province in Southeastern Anatolia, it is now grown throughout the country. Characterized by clusters of small, thick-skinned berries, this grape makes a wine as bold as its name (literally "burning throat") might imply. It is dark garnet in color and spicy on the nose with a finish that is long and strong. Single varietal Boğazkere wines are high in tannins and take oak very well, as those offered by Vinkara, Doluca (**DLC** Series), and Kavaklıdere (**Ancyra** Series) can testify.

Also native to Elazığ Province is the **Öküzgözü** (O-KOOZ-o-zoo) grape whose name means "Ox's Eye "or "Bull's Eye." Its large, dark berries and bright red juice produce wines that are aromatic and fruity (tart cherries and raspberries) with soft tannins. Doluca (**DLC** Series), Kavaklıdere, Kayra (**Vintage** Series) and Buzbağ (**Terra Anadolu Öküzgözü**) are all good examples of what this grape can do. Both Kavaklıdere and Turan use this grape to make a fortified (port method) wine. Blends that use the softer Öküzgözü to tame and temper the more tannic Boğazkere will produce wines in which the whole is much greater than the sum of its parts. Kayra's **Buzbağ Reserv** is just one of many great examples.

A BOOK TO LOOK FOR:

The Guide to Turkish Wines by Dr. Şeyla Ergenekon, a founder and member of the Istanbul Wine Tasting Society. It is difficult to find but – if you are successful – it is well worth the search.

Celebrate!

For special occasions there are several good sparkling (*köpüklü*) wines from which to choose. Kayra offers **Cameoş d'Oro**, a naturally sparkling wine from 100% Sultaniya juice. Both Kavaklıdere in its **Altın Köpük**, and Turasan in its **Special** Group, use Emir juice in their sparklers made by the Charmat process (secondary fermentation in bulk tanks). Vinkara was the first Turkish house to employ the French *méthode traditionelle* (secondary fermentation in the bottle) for its **Yaşasın**, a crisp *blanc de noir* from 100% Kalecik Karası grapes. It is perfect for any celebration.

Wine Bars & Bottle Shops

There are several spots in Istanbul where you can taste these Anatolian wines; these two are especially convenient.

Mehmet Yalçın, editor of *Gusto* magazine, and owner of Rouge Wine Bar.
Photo courstesy of the Time Traveling Gourmet.

Rouge Wine Bar can be found at Lamartin Caddesi 11/12, a pedestrian street off the upper end of Taksim Square. Truly an Alice's Restaurant for oenophiles, owner Mehmet Yalçin (editor of *Gusto* magazine) pays attention to every detail: from a *Le Verre de Vin* vacuum system for the more than 50 wines sold by the glass to a great menu of cheeses, charcuterie, and small plates to go with them. A bottle shop downstairs offers a wide selection of medal winners in bookshelf storage, with prices clearly marked. One caveat: check before you go, since there is talk that it may have closed after the recent troubles in neighboring Taksim Square.

Sensus Wine Boutique is located officially at Büyükhendek Caddesi 5 but, in actuality, it is in the basement of the Anemone Hotel directly opposite the Galata Tower which was built originally by the Genoese in 1348 as part of the city's defenses. Sample at the small bar or communal tasting table and then choose a bottle from the wide selection of Turkish wines from the shelves, crates, and baskets that surround you. You can't go wrong!

Constantine the Great, offering a model of the city of Constantinople to the Virgin Mary and Christ Child, is balanced on her right by the image of the Emperor Justinian who presents her with a model of Hagia Sophia (The Church of the Holy Wisdom). Hagia Sophia, Southwest entrance mosaic.
Photo by Myrabella (Wikimedia Commons, PD).

Sweet Tooth

At first glance *dondurma* may look like ice cream, but there is a big difference. Instead of using egg or corn syrup as a thickening agent, it uses *salep*, a flour ground from the dried tubers of a wild orchid (*Orchis masculis*), and a little *mastic* (resin) to provide elasticity. Dondurma is also great street theater, as your server will present your treat to you at the end of a long metal pole, always with great enthusiasm and flair. Try it, and savor the fun!

Pronunciation: The phonetic suggestions offered here are approximate and were worked out with the help of Mr. Taylan Sargin of the *Sensus Wine Boutique* to whom the author is extremely grateful. The pronunciation of Turkish words can be tricky. Watch out especially for the un-dotted I/ı (pronounced "eh") and the Ğ/ğ (that is not pronounced at all but rather lengthens the vowel in the preceding syllable).

Cheers!

In Istanbul,
just say

Limassol

Cyprus

e Port of Limassol is constantly being expanded and improved in order to accommodate the sharp rise in shipping that it serves.
oto by Hajotthi (WikimediaCommons, CC BY-SA 3.0).

East of the Akrotiri Peninsula, where the foothills of the Troodos mountains surrender to the sea, stands Limassol (Lemesós), the major port of the Republic of Cyprus and one of the busiest commercial ports in the editerranean. Exactly when humans began to walk these shores is uncertain, but chaeology suggests that it may have been as early as 10,000 BCE, possibly sharing e landscape with a strange menagerie of pygmy hippos and dwarf elephants.

nce there, however, humans quickly settled in, thriving on the fertility of the plain hile learning to exploit the rich and copious mineral resources of the hinterland. ief of these was copper (*kipros* in Greek), which gave its name to the island.

ound 3500 BCE, this new material had all but replaced stone in the primitive priote toolkit, a fact demonstrated at several excavations in the Limassol area. ne of these, in the little village of Erimi (eh-REE-mi), would present archaeologists th quite a surprise. After the residue from a small flask was analyzed by Drs. lgiorno and Lentini (CNR-ITABC, Rome), it was shown that not only were

This Cypriot copper *tetarterón*, bearing the image of crusader-king Richard I *(Cœur de Lion)*, was most probably minted shortly after his marriage to Berengária of Navarre in the tiny Chapel of St. George, Limassol, on May 12, 1191.
(Photo courtesy of Classical Numismatic Group, CNG 70, Lot 1148), http://www.cngcoins.com).

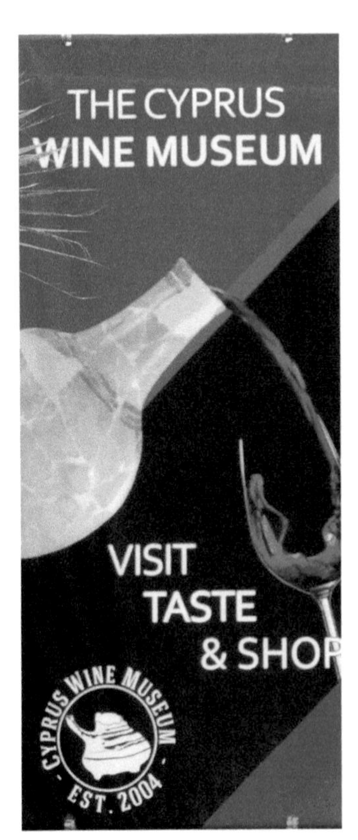

Wine symbolically pours into a modern wine glass from a 5,500 year-old flask excavated at the site of Erimi in this advertisement for The Cyprus Wine Museum on the outskirts of Limassol.
Photo courtesy of the Time Traveling Gourmet.

the villagers busy smelting copper, they were also hard at work making wine! This is the earliest evidence on the island for another product that would bring Cyprus fame and glory in later years.

Cyprus has always been a cultural crossroad. According to tradition, its population was augmented in the 12th century BCE by the diaspora of Greek warriors at the conclusion of the Trojan War, followed by Phoenician sailors and settlers beginning in the 9th century BCE.

Subsequently, Assyrians, Egyptians, and Persians each tried their hand at subjugating the local rulers until Alexander the Great arrived and pulled the island back from Persian control. However, the political turmo surrounding Alexander's death in Babylon a few years later (323 BCE) allowed Ptolemy, the general that he had installed in Egypt, to consolidate his control over the Eastern Mediterranean. And that included Cyprus! Local kingdoms were abolished and the island would remain a "Ptolemaic" possession until it was annexed by Rome in the year 58 BCE.

But incorporation into the expanding Roman orb would not bring peace to the island, and it was soon embroiled in the civil strife that gripped Rome after the assassination of Julius Caesar (44 BCE). Things came to a head when Marc Antony attempted to give Cyprus and other eastern territories to Cleopatra VII, and to legitimize Caesarion (her son by Julius Caesar). These actions led to the Battle of Actium (31 BCE) in which the shameful retreat of Antony and Cleopatra set the stage for their individual suicides and, four years later, for the demise of the Roman Republic and the birth of the Roman Empire under Octavian/Augustus.

Christianity was brought to Cyprus by Paul and Barnabas midway through the 1st century (Acts 12 & 13). And, while the literary record tend to be rather silent, archaeology gives us the impression of a high standard of living under Roman rule that would continue even after the Empire split and Cyprus became part of Byzantium. The island would remain more or less autonomous until 688, when the Byzantin Emperor Justinian II entered into an agreemer with the Umayyad Caliph Abd al-Malek

Limassol Marina is now the home port for the *Kyrenia Liberty*, a modern (2002) replica of a 4th century BCE Greek wine merchant's ship that sank near Kyrenia, off the northern coast of Cyprus. Excavation of the original ship was conducted by archaeologists Michael and Susan Katzev and a team from the Institute of Nautical Archaeology.
Photo courtesy of the Time Traveling Gourmet.

vhereby they would rule jointly ver a "neutral" Cyprus and oth would share the revenue rom taxes raised there. This nusual arrangement lasted lmost three centuries.

Kolossi Castle crowns a hilltop in the rich wine country of Limassol. Called *La Grande Commanderie* (garrison or military headquarters) by the Knights Templar, it has given its name to the sweet wine enjoyed in the area since the 8th century BCE.
Photo by Cun (Wikimedia Commons, PD).

s the 12th century ebbed, call or a Third Crusade rippled cross Europe forcing King ichard I of England (*Cœur e Lion*) to the forefront of he struggle as it dragged im deeply into Cypriot eopolitics. Sailing eastward cross the Mediterranean with is army and (on a separate hip) his fiancé, Berengária of avarre, the fleet was hit by a nonstrous storm that propelled Richard onward to Rhodes but drove Berengária's hip aground on Cyprus. Here she was taken hostage by Isaac Komnenos, then he quasi-legitimate king of the island. In retaliation, Richard put the island to the word and, in May of 1191, the couple was married in the Chapel of St. George in imassol. But Richard's heart was at home in England. He soon sold the island to the nights Templar who gave it back less than two years later, forcing him to pass it on o Guy de Lusignan, who had recently lost his claim to the Kingdom of Jerusalem. fter Guy died in 1194, Cyprus entered three centuries of rule y the French who continually fed the deepening animosity etween the Latin Catholic and Greek Orthodox churches.

leanwhile, a third element was added to the mix: the Muslim ulers of the Egyptian-based Mameluke (Mamluk) Sultanate. irst through conflict, and later by commercial cooperation, hey treated Cyprus much as a protectorate until 1473, when atherine, the last queen of Cyprus, was forced to abdicate. lthough Cyprus thus became a colony of Catholic Venice, he commercial relationship with the Mamelukes was so rofitable for both sides that it was allowed to continue .

Catherine Cornaro, the last queen of Cyprus. Portrait by Gentile Bellini.
Museum of Fine Arts, Budapest, Inv. no. 101. Photo by Yelkrokoyade (Wikimedia Commons, CC BY-SA 3.0).

Vhile Venice had been able to come to terms with the lamelukes this was not the case with the Ottoman urks who attacked and destroyed Limassol in 1539. And, hether it was to control Levantine trade or to insure his redilection for the already-famous wines of Cyprus, Sultan elim II (known as "Sultan the Sot") sent Turkish forces back to Cyprus in 1570 to lay siege to Nicosia. After only seven weeks the city capitulated, more than 20,000 of its citizens were slaughtered, and the Turks went on to destroy Famagusta with equal cruelty. Cyprus was now totally under Ottoman domination and would remain so for the next three centuries.

Alas, the modern history of Cyprus consists of more of the same. In 1878, through clandestine negotiations, the island became a ward of Great Britain with whom it would be associated, under a number of different rubrics, until the 1950s. Then the call for Cypriot "union" (*énosis*) with Greece erupted on the island which, in turn, was countered by demands for the "partition" (*taksím*) of the island into separate Greek and Turkish zones. Heated exchanges between adherents of the two positions raged through the 1960s until 1974, when Turkish forces invaded and seized over one-third of the island. Today, The Republic of Cyprus in the south is separated from The Turkish Republic of Northern Cyprus by a UN administered buffer zone. Talks continue.

The Local Grape Varieties

Because of its geographic isolation, Cyprus was spared the scourge of phylloxera that swept through Europe in the 19th century, and today it boasts some very old and rare vines. The "purity" of many of these varietals has been preserved through propagation via "callused cuttings" (*franc de pied*) that do not require them to be grafted onto disease-resistant, phylloxera-free (American) rootstock as is so often the case elsewhere. The island also enjoys a relatively dry climate that tends to discourage the growth of fungal diseases such as powdery mildew. No wonder its wines have been praised for so many centuries.

Until the 1980s, the commercial wine industry was dominated by four major wineries each identified by its Greek acronym. They are listed here by their date of founding: ETKO (1844), KEO (1926), LOEL (1943), and SODAP (1947). Traditionally, all of them produced their wines at factories in or near Limassol. To these giants can now be added the producers of what were once called "village" wines that were located closer to the vineyards and originally sold only in bulk. These have now been reclassified as "regional" wines and enjoy more government support. Yioskouris Winery is the oldest of these.

In 2004, after formal acceptance into the European Union, Cyprus initiated a regulatory system based on EU wine regulations (revised in 2007) that recognize three categories of wine from grapes grown in registered vineyards in four authorized geographic regions. The first category is Table Wine, a simple *vin de table* produced with a minimum of restrictions. Above this is Local Wine (*vin de pays*) for which a specific geographic region must be designated and from which, in most cases, 85% of the grapes must be sourced. The age of the vines and maximum yields are also stipulated. Above these, a superior category identified by its Greek acronym (O.E.O.Π.) on the label, further tightens vineyard management, adding higher altitudes, older vines, and smaller yields to the classification.

:gional wines may carry a regional indicator on their
bel but this merely indicates where the wine was made
ıd not necessarily where the grapes were grown. Feeling
at these controls are too restrictive many Cypriote
inemakers produce excellent wines outside the system.

/HITE GRAPES

ıe indigenous **Xynisteri** (Zin-eh-STER-ri) grape forms
e backbone of the island's white wine production as well
playing a major role in the blending of Commandaria
ee below). This grape is at its best when grown high above
massol, at the cooler levels of the Troodos Mountains. Here
veral producers craft mono-varietal, low alcohol (11–11.5%
3V) wines with a fresh and fruity nose and a wide range of
trus fruits and tart plum on the palate. Drink them chilled
–10C/46–50F) while still young (within the first year is best).

The Xynisteri grape.
Photo courtesy of the Monolithos winery, Cyprus.

ynisteri takes on a new dimension when exposed to
ık. Compare SODAP's Kamantérena Winery's **Arsinoe**
ith their slightly oaked **Paphos Dry White Wine**. Ktima
erolemo, in the legendary wine-village of Omodos, offers a
ynisteri Dryos** that has spent a longer time in (French) oak
rrels, while Xynisteri from Zambartas is even "oakier" and
gins to bend the flavor profile toward vanilla and cream
ıile extending its ageability. Xynisteri juice can also be
und blended with international grapes such as Malvasia,
millon, Gordo (aka Muscat of Alexandria), and Ugni Blanc.

:her traditional white grapes worth searching for are
e thin-skinned **Spourtiko** (Spur-ti-KO, "bursting"),
discovered and reintroduced by the Theodoros Fikardos
'inery, and **Promara** (Pro-MA-ra). Wines from field-
lected and hand-picked grapes of both varietals are made
the Vouni Panayia Winery in Paphos as part of their
ogram to preserve the indigenous grapes of Cyprus.

ED GRAPES

The Mavro grape.
Photo courtesy of the Monolithos winery, Cyprus.

ıe indigenous **Mavro** (MAV-ro, meaning "black") is
e most widely cultivated Cypriot grape, accounting
r up to 75% of all plantings. It bears ample clusters of
rge, almost table-grape sized, dark-skinned berries.
spite of (or perhaps because of) their size, wines made from them have low
id levels and are best consumed young when flavors of ripe (to candied)
erry and black currant predominate. Mono-varietal Mavro wines can

be found but the grape is most readily encountered in blends, especially Commandaria (see below). At the end of the harvest, Mavro skins and pomace are often distilled into the fiery, grappa-like spirit known as *Zivania.*

Maratheftiko grapes at harvest time. Photo by Cyprus Tourism CH (Wikimedia Commons, CC BY 2.0).

Maratheftiko (Ma-ra-THEF-ti-ko), also known as **Pampakia,** or **Vambakadha,** is a rare grape that represents less than 5% of the vines grown on the island, and i one of 12 indigenous varietals that were rediscovered by the late, KEO oenologist Akis Zambartas. It seems that the grape had been hiding in field blends where it may have been intentionally interspersed in order to add its more vibrant color, acidity, and tannins when blended with the juice of the lighter Mavro grape.

Because Maratheftiko is one of the few non-hermaphroditic grapes, it cannot self-pollinate and has difficulty setting its fruit (female flowers with reflexive stamens) and so it does better in environments where other varietals are on hand to assist. Zambartas Winery has enlisted Spourtiko (see above) to assist in this task because they both flower at about the same time. The same is done at the Vouni Panayia Winery.

Unfortunately, this grape is also extremely susceptible to bud loss which causes its yields to be even more limited, but it is an important and very versatile grape that is capable of bringing flavors of ripe cherry and blackberry to wines made in a variety of styles: from light rosés to those that will stand up to the heartiest fare.

By law, mono-varietal Maratheftiko wines must spend a minimum of six months in oak barrels that are less than three-year old, but this period is often extended as is the case with KEO's **Heritage** (14% ABV), Vouni Panayia Winery's **Barba Yiannis** (13% ABV), and Tsiakkas Winery's **Vamvakada** (13% ABV). Whether French, American, or a combination of oak is used, these wines are well-integrated and portend a tremendous future for the grape.

Ofthalmo (Of-THAL-mo), also known as Ophthalmo, is a low-yielding , traditional grape whose name is derived from the Greek/Latin word for "eye" with reference to the shape of its berries. It is a very dark, highly pigmented grape with low acidity, but more than the Mavro grape with which it is usually blended. KEO's **Othello** (Mavro/Ophthalmo) is a full bodied, fruity wine, with just a taste of oak, while similar "Dry Red" blends, such as that offered by Nelion Winery, present much more aggressive (cedar?) tannins.

Yiannoudi (Yah-NEW-thee), meaning "Yianni's", is another indigenous grape that, in spite of the pollination difficulties that it shares with Maratheftiko, has been recently reborn and regrown. Mono-varietal Yiannoudi wines are slowly becoming

Early Accolades for Commandaria

Year	Person	Praise
1191	Richard I Lionheart	"The wine of kings and the king of wines."
1224	Henry d'Andeli (Poet)	"The Apostle of Wines."
1363	The Lord Mayor of London	Served at the Banquet of the Five Kings
1576	Tomasso Porcacch (Scholar)	"...very luscious and wholesome..."
1819	Archbishop Constantius of Sina	"delicious ... the fragrant nectar of Zeus."

vailable with good examples from the KEO, Vouni Panayia, and Vasilikon wineries. siakkis Winery presents their offering as **Giannoudi**. Think Primitivo or Zinfandel.

̣elebrate!

f a wine was special enough to be served at the wedding of King Richard the ionheart, wouldn't it be perfect for your special event? **Commandaria** is he gem of Cypriot wines as it has been for centuries. It is a sweet, lush—even nctuous—wine that is achieved by leaving the fruit on the vine, or in the vineyard, ntil it has been dehydrated naturally by the sun. Praised as *Sweet Cypriote Jama* by classical authors, including Pliny and Strabo, instructions for making t were offered as early as the 8th century BCE by both Homer and Hesiod.

he higher level of alcohol achieved by using raisined grapes would have increased he "shelf life" of these wines, allowing them to be traded more widely as their eputation spread. And so it is not surprising that King Richard would have hosen the best for his wedding: the wine made nearby at the headquarters of the is knights: *La Grande Commanderie*. Such an endorsement, plus the acclaim of eturning travelers and the guile of Venetian merchants who awarded it tax-free tatus, combined to spread the reputation of this special wine across Europe. It thus ecame the first wine to have earned its own AOC (*appellation d' origine contrôlée*).

When Orion and Sirius rise to the middle of the sky...
Gather your grapes and bring them home.
Place them in the sun for ten days and nights,
Then in the shade for five and, on the sixth day,
Draw the joyous gift of Dionysos into your jars.

Hesiod, Works and Days (ll. 609–617); cf. Homer, *Odyssey* (VII: 140 ff.).

oday the production of Commandaria asically follows Hesiod's directions, utilizing Xynisteri and Mavro grapes dry-farmed n the fourteen specific villages in the interland of Limassol that make up the ommandaria Region. After a late harvest, the ruit is spread out in the sun to concentrate s sugars. Pressing and fermentation ollow, after which the wine may be moved ut of the region for mandatory aging in ak barrels. At this point the wine may be "fortified" with a small percentage f grape distillate in order to reach the desired level of residual sugar.

A Roman mosaic from the 2nd–3rd century Villa of Dionysos in nearby Paphos shows (L–R) Dionysos and his friend Acme enjoying a cup of wine as King Ikarios arrives with a wagon full of bulging wineskins. To the far right, as the caption tells us, are The First Wine-drinkers. Fearing that they had been poisoned by the strange effects of the new beverage, they later killed Ikarios
Composite of photos by Institute for the Study of the Ancient World, New York, United States of America (Wikimedia Commons, CC BY 2.0).

Wine Bars & Bottle Shops

At first glance, a recommendation for the *Wine Bar Italiano 100%* (at Odhos Safi 1) might seem out of place, were it not located in the building where, in 1844, Christos Hajjipavlou and his family brought the Cypriot wine and spirits industry into the modern age (note the proud dedication carved high on the side of the building). Here you can enjoy an excellent selection of quality Cypriot wines (many by the glass) as well as small plates (*meze*) to go with them. The *burrata caprese* alone is worth the trip. Off premises bottle sales are also available.

Other Limassol Attractions

If time permits, venture out to the wineries themselves along the well-marked Wine Routes that radiate from the urban centers. Two routes from Limassol explore the Commandaria villages. Or, if visiting during the autumn, attend the Wine Festival that has been held in the Municipal Gardens almost every year since 1961. And do not miss The Cyprus Wine Museum in the village of Erimi on the outskirts of Limassol, where the long history of wine is introduced by an informative, beautifully photographed film with music composed by Anastasia Guy, the museum's creator/director, and played by the museum's Commandaria Orchestra. After viewing the collection, enjoy a tasting of the museum's exclusive line of wines and zivania.

Cheers!

In Limassol,
just say

YIA-mas!

("To/For Us")

Málaga

Spain

ıe port of Málaga as seen from *El Castillo de Gibralfaro*, the ramparts that were built by the Nasrid King Yusuf I in 1340 in order to rn the heights into a fortress capable of protecting both the harbor and its town.

The Málaga coastline is dotted with caves that have sheltered the weary since the days of Paleolithic hunters and foragers. Recently the excavation of a campfire at one of these sites, Nerja, has provided archaeologists with tiny agments of marine barnacles. These were not ordinary barnacles but ones that e specifically associated with the Southern Right Whale (*Eubalena australis*), ıich commonly serves as their host. This suggests that as early as *c.* 12,000 :E, when local scavengers encountered one of these stranded behemoths, they uld harvest the more portable parts (skin, blubber, etc.) and bring them home complement the evening meal. Things changed, however, around 8,000 BCE as obal temperatures began to rise at the end of the Würm Glacial Period. Soon *E. stralis* would be lured southward by cooler waters, and culinary options on the erian Peninsula were replaced by those more suitable to the landscape of today.

A 3rd century BCE Málaga coin features the head of the god Hephaistos (Vulcan) behind which are depicted his tongs and the Phoenician letters *"mlk."*

Photo with the permission of wildwinds.com, ex-Numismatic Lanz.

was in this new setting that East met West at the dawn of the 8th century BCE. oenician merchants, whose relatives had provided King Solomon with the timber and talent to build his temple in Jerusalem, had arrived in the Bay of Málaga. They had sailed over 2000 miles to trade for the metallic ores that lay hidden in the Iberian hinterland. But it would not be all "take" by the newcomers, for the slopes of those mineral-rich hills would soon blossom with hearty varieties of the domesticated wine grape (*Vitis vinifera sativa*) that they had brought westward in their tiny ships.

Sporadic at first, these brief commercial visits developed into longer stays, eventually evolving into the colony known as *Málaka* after the rich deposits of salt (*mlk*) that were readily accessible along its shore. Salt was an essential element for the preservation of the fish and victuals needed on the long trip back across the Mediterranean, as well as to provision other ships for journeys out into the Atlantic, thought to have reached as far north as the Cornish Coast of England and as far south as the Gulf of Guinea.

The Liberation of the Captives of Málaga by the Catholic Monarchs (Ferdinand and Isabella), an oil on canvas by José Moreno Carbonero (*c.* 1930), illustrates the desperate plight of the Malagueños towards the close of the *Reconquista*.
Museo de Málaga (Wikimedia Commons, PD).

This arrangement worked well, and the Phoenicians soon came to dominate many of the sea lanes across the Mediterranean. This was especially true along its southern rim, as they competed with (and often confronted) Greek colonists staking out their own territories. Then, in 539 BCE, the Persian King Cyrus the Great defeated the Phoenicians in their homeland, leaving their overseas dependencies to fend for themselves. One of these, Carthage (modern Tunis), quickly took over the western colonies/trading posts (including Málaka) and forged them into an empire that would dominate the Western Mediterranean until it eventually butted heads with Roman expansion during the Punic Wars (264–146 BCE). The term Punic (Latin for "Phoenicians") stresses the Levantine ancestry of the Carthaginians.

Slowly and peacefully Latin *Málaca* came under Roman hegemony during the 2nd century BCE. Its position on the migratory route of tuna and mackerel, combined with the ability to move its products inland along the bustling *Via Herculea*, allowed Málaga to thrive during the years of the Roman Republic. The Emperor Domitian (ruled 81–96) even granted the right of citizenship to all free-persons through a special law (the *Lex Flavia Malacitana*). This was about the same time that a theater was constructed to provide entertainment for a population increasing in size and sensitivity to Roman culture.

Unfortunately, the good life in Roman *Málaca* was not to last. The Vandals arrived first, followed by a brief Byzantine interlude, and then a period of rule by the Visigoths during which time Nicene Catholics battled their Arian Christian countrymen over the true nature of the Divinity. That interfaith argument was halted quickly in 711 when Tariq Ibn Ziyad led an army of 7000 Berber soldiers across the Strait of Gibraltar, bringing seven centuries of Moslem rule to Al-Andalus. It was not until 1487 that these "Moors" were dislodged by the forces of Ferdinand and Isabella towards the end of the Christian *Reconquista*.

Perhaps the cruelest day in Málaga's long history occurred during the Spanish Civil War (February 7th, 1937), when its civilian population of *c.* 150,000 tried to flee on foot in the face of Generalissimo Franco's Nationalist army, augmented by the bombers of Hitler's Condor Legion. The ensuing massacre was vividly described in *El Crimen del Camino Málaga-Almería* written by Dr. Norman Bethune, an eye-witness who was serving there with a Canadian medical unit. A few months later bombs rained down on Guernica, further troubling the world with the senseless inhumanity of war and inspiring Pablo Picasso, Málaga's artist laureate, to create one of the greatest works of art of all time.

Today you can sit next to a statue of Picasso on a park bench in the Plaza de la Merced, less than a block from the artist's childhood home.

Málaga Wines

The wines of Málaga have two major *Denominaciones de Origen:* the first is *DO Málaga,* established in 1933 to regulate the traditionally-made sweet dessert wines. The second is *DO Sierra de Málaga* (2010) that covers the same geographic area but controls its off-dry, unfortified wines. When you choose a wine from either DO, you are actually selecting the type, or style, of the wine and the method by which it was made. Although the region is presently increasing its production of dry wines (mostly from international varieties often referred to as "Ronda Wines"), the traditional sweet wines of DO Málaga are emphasized here.

The Pedro Ximenez grape, often referred to as "Pedro," or simply "PX", is a stalwart of the Málaga DOC, but it was at one time thought to be identical to the German Elbling grape (pictured here).
Photo by Dr. Joachim Schmid (Wikimedia Commons, CC BY-SA3.0).

MÁLAGA WINE GRAPES

The two major grapes of DO Málaga are:

Pedro Ximenez (Hi-MEN-ez) is a thick-skinned, rather disease-prone white varietal that is widely grown in, and probably native to, Andalucía. Its naturally high sugar content can be further increased by drying in the sun which makes it ideal for blending in fortified wines, but single-varietal PX wines are also common. **Málaga Virgen PX** is a good example.

Moscatel de Málaga is one of many synonyms for the white grape more widely known as Moscatel de Alejandría (Muscat of Alexandria). It has a long history, but whether or not its origins can be traced back to the Egyptian city founded by Alexander the Great continues to be a matter of debate.

In addition, three minor grape varietals may also be encountered:

Lairén (AKA Malven, Malvar) is an obscure (evidently indigenous) Andalucían white grape that offers sufficient acid to make it welcome in fortified blends while also providing the necessary structure for a single-varietal wine. Recent DNA studies, however, have shown that it is not related to the Airén grape which is the most widely planted wine grape in Spain.

Doradilla is an historically elusive, white varietal with high sugar and low acid that is grown mainly in Andalucía.

Romé Tinto (AKA Romé Negro) is a light red grape that is also native and is now grown mostly in the Axarquía region of Málaga. Its lack of strong pigmentation makes it ideally suited to the dry varietal rosé produced by Bodegas Bentomiz as its **Ariyania Romé Rosado**.

An entire Roman theater was discovered accidentally in the center of Málaga in 1951 while landscaping work was being conducted along the lower slopes of the later Moslem Alcazaba (fortified citadel). Built in the 1st century during the reign of Emperor Augustus, the theater remained in use at least through the 3rd century.
Photo courtesy of the Time Traveling Gourmet..

The characteristic sweetness of DO Málaga wines is achieved by one or more of three processes (EU Regulation 753/2002), the borders between which are often hazy and thus the terminology used to describe them can be confusing.

- ***Asoleo*** ("sunbathing"), the oldest and simplest method, spreads late harvested grapes on straw mats *(paseros)* to let the sun further concentrate their sugars. This is similar to the French *vin de paille* ("straw wine").
- ***Arrope*** refers to unfermented grape juice that has been boiled down to a syrup and added to the must in order to achieve the desired level of sweetness. These wines can be described as *Vino Naturalmente Dulce* (i.e. naturally sweet) but are not considered to be fortified.

Mutage is the stopping (or "muting") of fermentation by adding a distilled spirit to the must. This method first required the discovery of distillation by Arab alchemists in Spain, sometime in the 8th century ("alcohol" = Arabic *al-kahul* means "the essence"). Arnaud de Villeneuve, a Valencian physician and translator of Arabic medical texts noted that, when alcohol was added to the must, it would kill the yeast and stabilize the residual sugars. These wines are called "fortified" and, in Málaga, they are described either as Maestro or Tierno depending upon when in the process the alcohol was added.

), prepare to be challenged as you p your way through the sweet wines Málaga, but isn't that part of the n? And to help you, note that wines ged in oak for at least six months ill be described as *Pálido*, while ose enjoying longer time in the rrel flaunt additional qualifiers: *oble* (2–3 years), *Añejo* (3–5 years), d *Trasañejo* (more than 5 years). s these wines age, their colors ill deepen: from *Dorado* (golden), rough *Rojo Dorado* (reddish gold) d *Oscuro* (brown), to *Negro* (black). e variety of styles is almost endless, nging from simply descriptive terms such as *Seco* (dry) or *Abocado* (medium dry), rough those with British-influenced names (Pale Dry, Cream, and Pale Cream) at seem more related to Fino, Amontillado and Amoroso Sherries. Two special tegories are: *Pajarete*, aged or naturally semi-sweet without either *arrope* or *utage*, and *Lágrima* ("tears"), a very sweet wine made only from free-run juice.

In a hurry? Conduct your own Málaga wine tasting later with a selection of sample-sized "minis" offered by Bodega Gomara and other wineries. From secco to sweet–with four stops in-between. Photo courtesy of the Time Traveling Gourmet..

he Solera System

) Málaga wines are often aged in an 18th century practice associated with e production of Sherry by which they are matured by fractional blending er an extended period of time. Traditionally, the barrels are arranged in a rtical pyramid. Then the new wine is added at the top and "trickles down" rough the successive tiers (*criadera* or "nurseries") to replace the wine that removed from the lowest tier (*solera* or "ground"). Modern technology allows is to be done horizontally in different rooms or even in separate buildings.

Vine Bars & Bottle Shops

sa Antigua de Guardia Alameda (at Alameda Principal 18) is the oldest and ost famous bar in Málaga. Choose from a dozen or so wines drawn directly

It is all about the basics at Casa Antigua de Guardia Alameda. They have been doing it this way since 1840.
Photo courtesy of the Time Traveling Gourmet.

Paloma Picasso, the youngest daughter of Pablo Picasso, and painter Françoise Gilot are just two of several celebrities who have signed their own barrel of Málaga wine at El Pimpi's bodega-bar.
Photo courtesy of the Time Traveling Gourmet.

from large barrels stacked behind the bar. Don't miss the **Isabel II**, a 100% *Moscatel de Alejandría trasañejo* (16% ABV), that has been aged for seven years in American oak. Queen Isabel enjoyed it so much during a visit there in 1862 that they named it after her. Prices are modest and your tab will be kept in white chalk on the bar in front of you. When you find the wine you like best you can take it home, in your bottle or theirs.

Another excellent spot at which to taste the wines of Málaga is *Bodegas el Pimpi* (Calle Granada 62 and the Jardines Alcazabilla). Established in 1971, this legendary bodega-bar feels much older, perhaps because it is housed in a building that once served as the stables of the 18th century Buenavista Mansion,and has also functioned both as a convent and a dance hall. Its history is proudly displayed in an endless series of photographs, while many local and international celebrities (Placido Domingo, Maribel Verdú, Antonio Banderas, etc.) have dropped by to autograph the darkened barrels that line its walls.

Not to be Missed

The *Museo del Vino* (Plaza de los Viñeros 1) offers a self-guided tour of artistically and educationally oriented exhibits that concludes with a modest tasting by an enthusiastic staff. Genuine!

Cheers!

In Málaga,
just say

(Sa-LOOD/T)

Rhodes

Greece

Mandraki Harbor, Rhodes – the modern statues of the stag *(élaphos)* and the doe *(elaphína)* are thought by many to mark the spot where the famous Colossus of Rhodes once stood: over 2000 years ago!
Photo courtesy of the Time Traveling Gourmet.

When Alexander the Great died in Babylon in June of 323 BCE, he pushed the Eastern Mediterranean World into a state of turmoil in which his strongest generals competed fiercely for dominance over segments of the largest empire that the world had ever known. Despite attempts to remain neutral, the island of Rhodes could not avoid being drawn into the conflict that would become known as the War of the Successors *(Diadochi)*. For Rhodes things came to a head in 305 BCE, when its citizens refused to give military assistance to the Macedonian general, King Antigonus I, during his war against another general, Ptolemy, who had taken control of Egypt. To punish Rhodes, Antigonus dispatched his son Demetrius, whose tactical use of complex military machines had won him the title of *Poliorcetes* ("The Besieger"), who quickly put his talents to work against the heavily fortified city and harbor. But even with a moveable, nine-story, metal-rmored tower on wheels named *Helepolis* ("The Destroyer of Cities"), bristling with atapults and ballistae, he could not breach the walls nor break the spirit of the city.

A silver Rhodian *tetradrachm* depicting the god Helios in all his solar glory.
Photo by CGB Numismatique Paris (Wikimedia Commons, CC BY-SA 3.0).

In less than a year Demetrius was forced to abandoned the siege, leaving his weapons and what remained of his incredible machinery scattered in heaps around the port.

From this chaos, life on Rhodes quickly returned to normal. International trade resumed and expanded, especially in its wine, already sufficiently famous to be discussed by Aristotle on his deathbed in 322 BCE (Gellius, *Attic Nights* 13.5.8). Rhodian amphoras are among the most frequently encountered—and most easily recognized—by archaeologists at sites all across the Mediterranean. Their handles are often stamped with an iconic rose (*rodhos* in Greek) or the head of Helios, and frequently include both the name of their maker and that of the eponymous magistrate by which the Rhodians kept their calendar.

The Colossus of Rhodes

Slowly, the citizens of Rhodes gathered the debris that Demetrius had abandoned—the Helepolis alone was said to have weighed 360,000 pounds—and they sold it as scrap for a handsome sum. This boon was used to commission a monument to celebrate their recent victory: a bronze *kolossos* (very large statue) of their sun god, Helios (the Roman Sol), who drove his horse-drawn (some say golden) chariot across the sky each day. Chares, a sculptor from the neighboring town of Lindos, and a pupil of the legendary sculptor Lysippos, began work in 292 BCE. He labored for the next 12 years until, either overcome by the magnitude of the project or the discovery of a costly miscalculation that left him bankrupt, Chares took his own life. Another Rhodian sculptor, Lache, brought the project to its conclusion.

The Colossus of Rhodes as it was conceived in the 16th century by the Dutch artist Maartin van Heemskerck, engraved and published by Philip Galle in 1572. Wikimedia Commons, PD.

Standing over 100 feet tall, roughly the same as New York's Statue of Liberty (111 ft, 6 in), it is the tallest statue that is known from antiquity and a fitting reason why many of the guidebooks of the day included it among the "wonders" *(thaúmata)* of their world. Standing atop a 50-foot base of marble, it would have been visible to ships far out to sea as it guided them to the safety and security of the harbor.

nfortunately, in 226 BCE Rhodes was ruck by a major earthquake. Buckling at e knees, the giant statue crashed down pon the town and harbor that it had once rved so well (Strabo XIV.2.9). Rhodes was gain covered by a pall of dust and rubble.

/hat were the people of Rhodes to do? The answer as not as clear as it was when they were dealing ith the spoils of an enemy. Helios was their god, d many thought the quake may have been a sign divine displeasure. And so, when Egyptian King olemy III (r. 246–222 BCE) offered to resurrect e monument, the Rhodians sought guidance from e famous Oracle at Delphi who advised them ot to rebuild lest they further offend their god.

The Palace (Kastello) of the Grand Master of Rhodes was subsequently used as a holiday escape by both King Victor Emanuel III and his Fascist successor Benito Mussolini.
Photo courtesy of the Time Traveling Gourmet.

he mighty had toppled. Throughout the nturies of Roman and Byzantine rule its mains would lay where they had fallen. But it ould not rest in seclusion. It's sheer size, one the features that placed it high on the bucket st of many an ancient traveler, continued to aw admirers even in its state of fragmented pose. Such respect was not shown by everyone. ortly after Caliph Muawiyah and his Umayyad armies conquered Rhodes in 54, the remnants of the statue were collected, melted down, loaded onto 900 mels, and taken to market for sale. Its final disposition remains a mystery.

Rhodian Wines

fter centuries of exporting a quality product across the Mediterranean, the putation of Rhodian wines began to falter. There was a brief respite after the land fell to the Knights of St. John of Jerusalem in 1310, but this faded after ileiman the Magnificent drove the Hospitallers from the island two centuries ter. Wine production is said to have been sporadic during the years that the land served as the center of an Ottoman province *(sanjak)*, but this trend ould reverse itself in the early 1900s. The end of the Italo-Turkish War had ought peace and had also attracted an influx of Italian farmers, many of hom brought their knowledge—and their root stock—with them. In 1928, e *Compagnia Agricola Industriale Rodi* (C.A.I.R.) was formed by a group Italian investors and the modern Rhodian wine industry was born.

oday the Rhodian wine industry is thriving, especially near the village of nbonas (Emponas) on the slopes of Mt. Attavyros. There the combination of isolation and altitude had protected many vineyards from the scourge of phylloxera as it slowed its march across the Dodecanese Islands in the late 19th century. One can still find patches of self-rooted vines (i.e. those not grafted onto American root stock)—especially of the Athiri grape—at these higher levels.

In the 1970s Greece adopted and adapted the European Union's system of wine classification, which has been greatly simplified in recent years. The wines of Rhodes can now be discussed according to either of two PDO (Protected Designation of Origin) appellations: "PDO Rhodes" (for dry white or dry red/rosé wines), or "PDO Muscat of Rhodes" (for sweet white wines). Rhodian wines can also be bottled as a PGI (Protected Geographical Indication) with more flexible and less stringent requirements. Regulations for Rhodian *souma*, the grappa-like beverage made from grape pressings and *marc* (pomace) that have been boiled in wine for about 20 days before distillation, also appear to be more flexible.

WHITE GRAPES

White PDO Rhodes wines must contain a minimum of 70% juice from the **Athiri** (Ah-THER-I) grape, an ancient varietal whose name suggests an origin on the island of Thera (Santorini), but one that has been grown so successfully here that it is often simply referred to as "Rhodes" on many wine labels. The grape produces a fragrant, delicate (yet lively) wine whose medium acidity recalls Meyer lemon, especially when grown on the higher elevations of Mt. Attavyros. Good introductions to this grape are the single varietal Athiri wines offered by Kounaki Winery, Enoteca Emery (single vineyard), and C.A.I.R.'s **Athiri Rodos 2400**. Compare/contrast these with the smokier wines from the self-rooted Athiri vines offered by the Alexandris Winery in Embonas.

The Athiri grape, a popular varietal grown on several of the Aegean Islands, is the main work horse of Rhodian white wine production.

Photo from *The Cretan Grapes* by Maritina Stavrakaki and Manolis N. Stavrakakis, Tropi Publications, Athens. Used with the permission of the authors.

The appellation also allows the softer Athiri to be blended with the more acetic **Assyrtiko** (Ah-SEER-ti-ko) grape as is also done on Santorini (which may be this grape's birthplace as well), in order to add a flinty minerality to the mix. **Malagouzia** (Ma-la-goo-ZYA), another versatile white grape, may also be included in the blend. This grape was saved from near extinction at the experimental village in Porto Carras in northern Greece (Chalkidiki) where it was replanted after being identified in western Greece (Nafpaktos) in the 1970s. Now planted widely, the grape is especially popular on the island of Rhodes. Single varietal Malagouzia wines, such as that offered by Kounaki are fragrant and fruity (peach, pear, and even banana) often with surprisingly low alcohol (11%).

By law, the sweet PDO Muscat of Rhodes wines may be crafted from either of two white varietals. The first is **Muscat Blanc à Petit Grains**, a small-berried member of ıe Muscat family that may have been grown on the island since antiquity and ; often referred to simply as Muscat Blanc or Moschato Aspro. The second ; the **Moscato di Trani**, a grape introduced from the eastern coast of Italy ither by the Knights of Rhodes when they ruled the island, or by Italians rom the vicinity of Trani (Apulia) during their occupation of the Dodecanese 1912–1947). These two clones are thought to be related, but the exact nature f that relationship is beyond the scope of this short introduction.

weet wines may be identified further as *vin naturellement doux (VND)*, if the grapes ave been sweetened by post-harvest sun/air drying, or either *vin doux naturel VDN)* or *vin de liqueur* if the sweetness is the result of grape spirit being added uring the fermentation process. For a starter, try Kounaki Winery's (monovarietal) Aosxato Rodou whose semi-raisined grapes build complex flavors and push ıe alcohol level to 16 %. Inclusion of the phrase *"grand cru"* on a label signifies nly that the wine is the product of a small-yield, privately-owned vineyard.

RED GRAPES

ed PDO Rhodes wines must contain a minimum of 70% juice rom the grape locally called **Amorgiano** (A-mor-JYA-no). This ; actually the same grape that is known as **Mandilaria** on rete but is so-called on Rhodes because the grape was thought ɔ have originated on the neighboring island of Amorgos. ts clusters of deep, intensely red (some say "black") berries re high in acid with potentially rigid tannins. Kounaki ıakes a full-bodied, deep red, monovarietal Amorgiano vine (PGI) redolent with ripe strawberries and cherry ım. The grapes spend about a week spread out under the hodian sun before they are pressed into a 14.5% ABV flavor omb! Amorgiano/Mandilaria may also be blended with a ıaximum of 30% **Mavrothiriko** (Ma-vro-THER-i-ko) ("Black thiri") juice. This grape thrives in the warm lowland lains of Rhodes (Zone A), producing complex wines with deep ruby color that are low in acid and high in alcohol.

A cluster of Amorgiano grapes, the major red wine varietal of the PDO Rhodes appellation, is also known as Mandilaria elsewhere in Greece.

Photo from *The Cretan Grapes* by Maritina Stavrakaki and Manolis N. Stavrakakis, Tropi Publications, Athens. Used with the permission of the authors.

Wine Bars & Bottle Shops

n Rhodes City, the *Cellar of Knights*, tucked under the Public ibrary in Syntrivani (Fountain) Square, proudly flaunts its ɔng history. During the 14th century this building served s the administration center (*Kastellania*) for the Knights of hodes and today it does a remarkable job in offering its customers the opportunity ɔ taste practically any wine or spirit made on the island. If wine-tasting around the illage of Emponas, a wide selection of local wines is available for either the tasting r the taking at the *Traditional Kiosk Emponas* located right in the center of town.

Celebrate!

The first widely-distributed sparkling wine in Greece was produced on Rhodes by the legendary C.A.I.R. Winery and the island still produces a surprising number of sparkling wines including those made by the traditional *champenoise* method (secondary fermentation in the bottle) and those made by the Charmat method (secondary fermentation in a tank). Both types have been included in the PDO Rhodes appellation since 2011. C.A.I.R. offers the widest selection of sparklers that use traditional grapes, including both a brut and a demi-sec each made from 100% Athiri. Keep an eye out for their **Rosé Reserve** (Mandilaria and Muscat Trani) and a very tasty **Brut Black** (Mandilaria and Athiri). The Kounaki Winery blends Athiri and Malagouzia in its **Sparkling White Demi-Sec Wine** which is also made in the classic manner.

Local wines for sale at Manolis Bakis' Taverna at the entrance to the village of Emponas.

Get Thee To A Winery

(A personal note)

Because the author's most recent visit to Rhodes was limited to a brief stop on a cruise ship, I decided to take a personal wine tour offered by **Rhodes Private Tours.** Their arrangements allowed me to visit and taste at several excellent wineries (Mrs. Anastasia, Emery, Merkouris, Kounaki, and Alexandris) and still be back on the ship for sail out. They were terrific and I would recommend them to anyone! Further information is available on their Web site, and note that you must pay in cash—which I did! And make certain that you include lunch at Manolis Bakis' *Taverna* at the entrance to the village of Emponas. It was founded in 1903 by the same family that still serves the best *paidakia* (lamb chops) on the island.

Cheers!

In Rhodes,
just say

YIA-mas!

("To/For Us")

Santorini

Greece

crisp white wine in a sea-blue bottle by the Gavalas Winery perfectly captures the predominant colors of the Greek island of ntorini. Looking out across the caldera from Petros Matekas' Villa Renos.
oto courtesy of the Time Traveling Gourmet.

Tradition tells us that the island we call Santorini or Thera today was also known by two names in antiquity: Strongilos ("the round island") and Kalliste ("the most beautiful island"). It was a rich and fertile land whose eople enjoyed a high level of sophistication, one on a par with the Minoan vilization that flourished on the neighboring island of Crete. And it may, in fact, ave been a Minoan colony.

Lacking an identifiable currency of their own, the people of ancient Thera relied on the coinage of neighboring Aegean islands such as this silver *stater* from Aegina dated to the second half of the 4th century BCE.
Photo courtesy of Classical Numismatic Group, Triton XXI, Lot 424. https:www.cngcoins.com.

odern interest in the island and its volcano can be traced back to the 1860s when French geologist, Ferdinand Fouqué, began a study to determine whether the ımice from the Santorini volcano could be used to make the siliceous (pozzolanic) ment required to build the Suez Canal. While he was there, Fouqué excavated chitecture and bits of ancient pottery, but at that time neither their age—nor eir importance—were understood. Knowledge of these finds percolated through e archaeological world for decades until University of Athens Professor yridon Marinatos brought them into historical focus while excavating a Iinoan" villa on the north coast of Crete, just 85 miles south of Santorini.

The excavations at Akrotiri can be viewed easily from the raised walkway that runs throughout most of the site.
Photo courtesy of the Time Traveling Gourmet.

Marinatos' finds reinforced his long-held theory that it had been a *tsunami* generated by the eruption of the volcano on Strongilos that caused the destruction of the cities and towns of Minoan Crete. Accordingly, in 1967, he moved his research to Santorini, where he would work at the site of Akrotiri for the rest of his life. He died and was buried there in 1974, but the spectacular finds he discovered, as well as those subsequently unearthed by Professor Christos Doumas and others, have brought to light the remains of a wealthy and vibrant community. It was one that had very much in common with its Minoan neighbors to the south.

For those living on that beautiful island, *la dolce vita* came to an abrupt and terrifying end sometime during the middle of the second millennium BCE. After a volcanic eruption many times more powerful than the one that destroyed Krakatoa, the bottom literally fell out of their island—and their lives. In a nightmare of choking gas and flaming pumice, most of Strongilos simply vanished! Many believe that memory of this cataclysmic event is preserved in two of Plato's dialogues (*Timaeus* and *Critias*) where we read that "in a single day and night of misfortune" the island-continent of Atlantis "disappeared into the depths of the sea."

A two-handled pouring vessel excavated at Akrotiri, decorated with one of the earliest representations of grape clusters, dates to the 17th century BCE.
Museum of Prehistoric Thera. Photo courtesy of the Time Traveling Gourmet.

It is uncertain how long the fertile fields of Strongilos lay fallow after this catastrophe, but at some point they caught the eyes of Phoenician traders/settlers as they expanded westward from their Levantine homeland. Herodotus (*Histories* IV.147) tells us that they had been settled there for eight generations before the arrival of Dorian colonists from mainland Greece, led by a man named Theras. After this event, usually assigned a date in the 9th century BCE, the island would become known as Thera (Thira).

The subsequent history of Dorian Thera is marked by a series of ups and downs: mostly the latter. The island played only a minor—and intermittent—role in the geopolitics of the Classical Period. However, it was able to boast a century of relative prominence after it became home to a large contingent of the Ptolemaic navy in the second half of the 3rd century BCE. An impressive building boom ensued, complete with civic buildings, a theater that could hold almost 1500 spectators, and even a sanctuary for the Egyptian gods (Osiris, Isis, and Anubis) who were honored by many of the sailors stationed there. Unfortunately, when the fleet left, so did this source of the island's prosperity.

uring the first century, the Romans remodeled the theater ccording to the fashion of the day, erecting an elaborate rchitectural background, known as a *scanae frons,* and decorating with statues of the imperial family. Later, Roman historian Cassius io, writing in the 3rd century (*History* LXI.7), noted that in the ear 47 a new island appeared in the middle of the caldera. This ould later become known as *Kameni* ("the burnt one). However, e reason that Roman Thera enjoyed only marginal importance as its isolated position on the western edge of the province of Asia *Asiana)*—and its volcano! This situation continued throughout e Byzantine Period. Decline continued slowly until 726, when e volcano erupted again. Once more the island was covered by a tifling pall of pumice. Such has life been on the island. As political ontrol passed from Genoese to Venetians to Nazi Germans (to ame a few), substantial seismic activity has occurred on at least dozen occasions. A new island, Nea Kameni ("the new burnt ne"), appeared in the caldera to the north of what would then ecome known as Palia Kameni ("the old burnt one"). Although the olcano is still classified as active, the most recent eruption was the onth-long flare-up of Nea Kameni in 1950. It has been quiet since.

A self-portrait and the depiction of a dolphin in honor of Poseidon. A man named Artemidoros carved these reliefs in the open-air sanctuary he built in Ancient Thera in the 3rd century BCE.
Photo by Olaf Tausch (Wikimedia Commons, CC BY-SA 3.0).

uring these centuries of uncertainty, the faithful of the island have demonstrated special devotion to Saint Irene (Agia Irini), the youngest of three sisters who ere martyred during the reign of the Emperor Diocletian (284–305). Thera's lternate name, Santorini, is a contraction (or elision) of her Latinized name Santa + Irini). It is first encountered in print (as *Santurin*) in the writings of the 2th century Moslem geographer al-Idrisi. Variants of her name appear on many arly maps, identifying a basilica dedicated to her in the village of Perissa, and 15th century Venetian chapel on the small island of Thirassia in the caldera.

Santorini winemakers create miracles from grapes grown amid the sterile pumice and fist-sized chunks of glassy lava that many believe are all that remains of the mysterious lost continent of Atlantis.

Viniculture

hrough it all, the people of Santorini have developed a tenacity that has stood hem well. This strength is evident in their ability to craft quality wines from rapes grown in soil so hostile that even the blight of phylloxera chose to pass the land by. Further complicating the situation is the fact that Thera has no water! nd what little rain it gets comes only during the winter months when the vines re dormant. After that, as the heat builds throughout the spring and summer, e parched vines must survive on whatever moisture they can extract from e humid air, and morning dew deposited on their leaves by evaporating sea ater. Over the centuries, however, local growers have learned to protect their n-grafted vines by weaving the canopy of each into what looks like a circular bottomless) basket called a *kouloura* (pl. *kouloures*). There, protected from the ual scourge of intense heat and searing wind, the grapes can ripen safely.

The volcanic terroir of Thera is bleak at best.
Photo courtesy of the Time Traveling Gourmet.

In 1971, recognizing the unique relationship between three indigenous Santorini white grapes, the island's unique *terroir,* and the specific vinicultural techniques practiced on the island, the European Union granted the island's wines an Appellation of Origin of Superior Quality (similar to the French *Vin de Qualité Produit Région Déterminée*) which has since been simplified to a PDO (Protected Designation of Origin) system. This recognition rejuvenated winemaking on the island.

Once begun, change came rapidly, just in time to appeal to the waves of tourists that were beginning to descend upon the island. In 1988, Yannis Boutaris brought his family's century of winemaking experience to the island and built a state-of-the-art winery in the village of Megalochori. There they joined historic, local icons such as Canava Roussos, the oldest winery on the island (founded in 1836) and Canava Argyrou (established in 1903). In 1992, Santo Wines, a 1200-member agricultural cooperative formed in 1947, completed an ultra-modern winery on the caldera in the village of Pyrgos, and quickly became the largest wine producer on the island. These years also saw the arrival on the Santorini wine scene of Yannis Paraskevopoulos (Gaia Winery) where his University of Bordeaux credentials have served him well both as a winemaker and a consultant.

The fusion of modern techniques, imported talent, and a home-grown understanding of the island's unique *terroir* works miracles on Santorini, producing wines that are attractive to the modern palate, while at the same time honoring and respecting the history of the island.

Equally as important as modernization has been its integration with the vast storehouse of knowledge built by those who have worked the island's harsh *terroir* for generations. George Gavalas, Jr., began making wine under the watchful eye of his 90-year-old father in a 300-year old building in the village of Phira. His grapes are mechanically crushed, cold fermented in stainless steel tanks, and bottled in iconoclastic blue glass bottles. Or there is Paris Sigalas, a local math teacher who had made wine at his home by the sea in Oia (EEE-ya) for years before moving into the modern winery that he had built next door (1998). When the *Wine Spectator* conducted a tasting of 15,000 international wines in an attempt to identify the 100 best wines released in 2007, his blend of two indigenous Santorini grapes appeared as number 96!

WHITE GRAPES

Archaeologists have shown that the wine grape *(Vitis vinifera)* has flourished on Santorini since at least 5000 BCE, while DNA analysis has identified more than fifty grapes that are either indigenous or traditional to the island. The three varietals that are permitted in wines of the PDO Santorini appellation are all white: Assyrtico, Aidani, and Athiri, and are used to produce wine in two styles: dry white wines and the sweet wine popularly known as Vinsanto.

law, the appellation "PDO Santorini – Dry White" ines must contain a minimum of 75% Assyrtico with the maining portion being made up of Aidani and/or Athiri. e use of oak is at the discretion of the winemaker.

The Assyrtico grape is the backbone of the PDO Santorini wines. This photo is from *Ampelography* by Manolis N. Stavrakakis, Tropi Publications, Athens (in Greek).
Photo courtesy of Manolis N. Stavrakakis.

ssyrtico (Ah-SEER-tee-co), Assyrtiko in Greek, is the ckbone of the Santorini wine industry, and may have been ought to the island by the Phoenicians 3000 years ago. Today s highly valued for its ability to survive hot summers while taining its crisp acidity. To capture its essence, try one of ese monovarietal wines. Artemis Karamolegos Winery oduces **Pyritis** from small plots of self-rooted vines that are imed to be over 120 years old. Another of their Assyrtico nes won a Best in Show medal at the Decanter World Wine vards in 2018. Gaia Wine's **Thalassitis** (roughly translated "sea born") is produced from the fruit of 80 year old vines an ultra-modern winery in a renovated, historic (PDO-ntorini) tomato cannery near Kamari Beach. It has been e of the most consistently successful wines ever produced the island. And, for a little geographic diversity, there is omaine Sigalas' **Epta**, a limited-edition collection of single ttles from each of seven *(epta)* different Santorini villages.

has been said that Assyrtico is a white grape that believes it is a red grape, and that respect it takes well to oak aging. Fruit from century-old vines is fermented d aged in French oak in Santo Wines' **Santorini Assyrtiko Grande Reserve**. ia Wines' **Thalassitis Wild Ferment** utilizes both French and American oak as ll as French acacia barrels. Estate Argyros' **French Oak Fermented** has been nsidered by *Decanter* to be the best dry, white, single varietal wine in the world!

dani (Eye-THAN-nee) is a rare local grape that is most often used in blends complement the structure and balance the potential sharpness of Assyrtico. onovarietal Aidani wines (designated PGI Cyclades) include Argyros' **Aidani** ade from dry-farmed, 50-year-old vines grown on the slopes of Mt. Episkopi, d Karamolegos' **Aidani** from younger (25-year-old) vines from a selection of neyards. The grape was also grown organically by the late Haridimos Hatzidakis a vineyard that he resurrected after it had been abandoned after the 1956 rthquake. Look for his **Aidani** 2014 whose label is a whimsical drawing by his (then e-school) daughter Stella, who will hopefully continue his work at the winery.

thiri (Ah-THIR-ee) is another ancient grape, one whose name attests to a long d strong connection with the island. Despite its low to moderate acidity, it ings a balancing, lemony-citrus flavor to the wines with which it is blended.

e "PDO Santorini – Sweet Wine" appellation covers Vinsanto, the island's ditional sweet wine that is often confused with Vin Santo ("Holy Wine"),

Mandilaria (Amorgiano) is a black, highly tannic grape that produces monovarietal wines that are very rich in color, but low in alcohol.

Photo from *The Cretan Grapes* by Maritina Stavrakaki and Manolis N. Stavrakakis, Tropi Publications, Athens. Used with the permission of the authors.

which is made in Tuscany from dried grapes (Trebbiano Toscana and Malvasia Bianca). This has led to considerable argument over the place of origin of wines made in this manner. In 2002 the European Union gave this honor to Santorini because its grapes are dried in the sun. It alone is allowed to call such wines Vinsanto (one word), while Italian versions must be referred to as Vin Santo, Vino Santo, etc.

Vinsanto is built upon a minimum of 51% Assyrtico juice. The remaining 49% may be made up of Aidani and/or Athiri with—perhaps—a very small percentage of juice from other island varietals. At harvest, the grapes are spread out in the August sun for 12–14 days or until the concentration of sugars measures at least 370 gr/l. After pressing, the wine should be aged for a minimum of two years in oak barrels. If longer aging is desired, then it must be done in multiples of four years. Vintages may be blended but the labeling should record the date of the most recent harvest.

The addition to the label of the phrase *vin naturellement doux* indicates that concentration was accomplished through natural means, i.e. by drying in the sun, and it may also be referred to as a *vin liastos* (straw wine). If the label reads *vin doux naturel* it is still a natural wine, but one that has been fortified through the addition of a wine-based alcohol *(vin de liquor)*.

NYKTERI

Also included in the PDO-Santorini appellation are wines referred to as *Nykteri*, a term that recalls the local tradition of picking and processing the grapes in the cool of the night *(nikta)*. Ultra-ripe grapes with a high sugar content can be vinified in either stainless steel or oak, after which they must spend a minimum of three months in oak barrels. The resulting wine must be a minimum of 13.5% ABV. Excellent monovarietal Assyrtico examples include Xatzidakis' **Nykteri** that is aged in oak for 12 months, and Sigalis' **Nychteri Grand Reserve** that spends a longer time in the barrel. Santo Wines blends all three of the PDO Santorini grapes (Assyrtico, Aidani, and Athiri) in their **Nykteri Reserve** and then ages the results for nine months in oak barrels plus three more months in the bottle. You may also encounter the term "Mezzo." While not a legal term according to the Greek classification system, it is ofte used for variants that are made in a manner similar to Vinsanto but are less sweet.

RED GRAPES

Wines from the red grapes of Santorini have not, at present, been given PDO status and often you will find them labeled PGI Cyclades (i.e. Regional wines of Cyclades). Again, three varietals are most frequently used in the red wines of Santorini.

⁄Iandilari(a) (Man-di-LAH-ri (-ya), nown by different names elsewhere n the Aegean Islands (Amorgiano on he island of Rhodes) is a black, highly annic grape that produces monovarietal vines that are very rich in color, but ow in alcohol. As a result, the grape s most often encountered in blends.)n Santorini the blending grape of hoice is Mavrotragano (see below), ut Volcan Winery blends a little Mandilaria (plus/minus 20%) with its ssyrtico to produce its **Lava Rosé**, as oes Domaine Argyros for its **Atlantis Rosé**. Both are perfect quaffing wines or a Santorini summer afternoon.

Two manikins at the Koutsogiannopoulos Family Wine Museum demonstrate work on the wine press on the island decades ago.
Photo courtesy of the Koutsogiannopoulos Family Wine Museum at the Volcan Winery.

Mavrotragano (Ma-vro-TRAG-a-no), from *mavro* (black) and *traganó* (crisp/ runchy) is a thick-skinned, small berried grape that ranges in color from a eep red to black. Indigenous to Santorini, the grape was traditionally blended nto wines such as Vinsanto and Nykteri. Slowly losing ground to the higher- ielding Assyrtico, it began to fade almost to extinction. Surviving mostly in eld blends, it now represents only 2–3% of the grape plantings on the island, ut new plantings are increasing thanks to the popularity of the grape.

lthough frequently used in blending, especially with Mandilaria, the recent ocus has been on developing a dry, monovarietal Mavrotragano wine. This hallenge was pioneered by Paris Sigalas and Haridimos Hatzidakis at their espective wineries. In addition, Santo Wines and Gavalas Winery now produce xcellent examples. Karamolegos Winery adds a modern twist in the vineyard y training its Mavrotragano vines on vertical wire and pruning them in the i-lateral Guyot system. All of these programs include some time in oak to keep he tannins soft and manageable. Together these wineries have called attention a grape that was near extinction just a few years ago, but the grape has ow developed a degree of cult status having been "adopted" by Slow Foods, ncouraging its protection. This rise in popularity has been mirrored by a ise in price, but it is a match made in heaven for lamb and eggplant dishes.

Mavrathiro (Mav-RATH-i-ro) is a very old and rare grape whose name means lack (*mavro*) Athiri. It has also survived the years by hiding in field blends vith other grapes. The spirit of these wines is captured nicely by Canava oussos' **Mavrathiro** where it is blended with Assyrtico and Mavrotragano to roduce a jammy and spicy dessert wine. All of the grapes are harvested late nd dried further in the sun, concentrating flavors and making it a true *vin ouge doux de passerillage*, with 11.5–12.5% ABV. It is sold in 50 cl bottles.

A perfect view of the caldera can be had at *The PK Cocktail Bar.* It is named after Palia Kameni, the small island in the background that was first mentioned by a Roman historian in the year 47. The statue is a plaster cast of the Venus de Milo (2nd century BCE), the original of which is in the Louvre.
Photo courtesy of the Time Traveling Gourmet.

Celebrate!

When only "the bubbly" will do, Santo Wines offers you two choices: a sparkling rosé blend of Assyrtico and Mandilaria, and a monovarietal Assyrtico that is released in both standard 750 ml, as well as convenient 200 ml bottles. Both are made in the classical method (secondary fermentation in the bottle). Another choice might be one of Artemis Karamolegas' semi/demi-sparkling wines. Their **Pnoé White** is a very interesting blend of the three traditional Santorini white grapes, along with Platani, Kritiko, and Katsani. The **Pnoé Rose** blends the two Santorini red grapes and also adds the juice of Voudomato grapes. *Pnoé* (Pnow-AY) is the Greek word for " breath" or "wind."

We may never know for certain whether the cataclysm that rocked the beautiful island of Strongilos actually did serve as the inspiration for Plato's intriguing story of the lost continent of Atlantis, but it is a fascinating possibility to ponder while sipping a glass of Santorini wine and watching the sun melt slowly into Homer's "wine dark" sea.

A Santorini Must-See

Oenophiles visiting the island should not miss the Wine Museum at the Volcan Winery on the road to Kamari Beach (accessible by public bus). Here, in their centuries-old wine caves, the Koutsogiannopoulos family has collected all manner of local wine-making tools and other paraphernalia that date back to the 1600s. These items are brought to life by a cast of manikins who demonstrate how the various pieces were used. Take your time with an automated, self-guided audio tour in your choice of 14 languages (or a guidebook in 22) and top it off with a tasting of several of Volcan's fine wines, all of which are included in the modest admission price.

For Further Reading: Stavroula Korakou, *Vinsanto: The Traditional Sweet Wine of Santorini,* Foinikos Publications, Athens (GR). ISBN 978-960-6849-53-4.

Cheers!

In Santorini,
just say

YIA-mas!

("To/For Us")

Taormina

Sicily, Italy

ount Etna looking down upon the Bay of Naxos as seen from the 3rd century BCE theater at Taormina.
to by Evan Erickson (Wikimedia Commons, PD).

Geologists tell us that Mount Etna (also Aetna) has gazed down upon the Bay of Naxos for hundreds of thousands of years. With a name derived from the ancient Phoenician word for furnace *(attuna)*, the smoking summit Europe's most active volcano became the setting for some of antiquity's most eresting dramas. Hesiod says that it was the location of the forge and workshop Hephaistos (Roman Vulcan) as well as home to the giant, one-eyed Cyclopes who d fashioned both Zeus' thunderbolt and Poseidon's trident. Homer and Virgil both ntified the mountain as the lair of another group of Cyclopes: the cannibalistic rdsmen whose leader, Polyphemus, devoured so many of Odysseus' crew *lyssey* IX, *Aeneid* III, *Georgics* IV). Such a rich mythological heritage, combined th its distinctive profile, would have made Etna a welcome navigational beacon early seafarers as they plied the waters of the Western Mediterranean.

The wine-god Dionysos wearing a wreath of ivy appears on the obverse of a *drachma* minted at Sicilian Naxos towards the end of the 6th century BCE.
Photo courtesy of Classical Numismatic Group (80532), http://www.cngcoins.com.

d so, in 734 BCE, Etna would have observed the ships of a small group Chalcidian Greek colonists led by an Athenian named Theocles,

The reverse of the same coin bears a cluster of grapes and the word "NAXION," indicating that it was minted by that Sicilian colony.
Photo courtesy of Classical Numismatic Group (80532), http://www.cngcoins.com.

under the patronage and protection of the god Apollo, as they took shelter in the small bay to the north of the Alcantara River, and stepped ashore. This would become Naxos, the first Greek colony in Sicily.

To celebrate their safe arrival, the colonists climbed the lava flow to the rocky outcropping of Cape Schisò, and erected an altar to their divine founder, Apollo Archegytes, in his guise as leader and protector of colonies. Thucydides (VI.3) noted that the altar would become the mandatory first and last stop for all official envoys going to (or returning from) Greece.

The little colony proved to be very successful and soon its members expanded inland with Theocles founding neighboring Leontini (modern Lentini) less than five years later. What financed this expansion is unknown but the popularity of grape clusters and images of the god Dionysos on early Naxian coinage provide us with a hint. *Vitis vinifera* still thrives on the rich volcanic soils of Giardini Naxos, spewed from the heights of the towering volcano.

Perhaps it was this wealth that brought on the decades of internecine squabbles with their Sicilian neighbors, hostilities that were only compounded by the colony's support of Athen's ill-fated Sicilian Expedition. Things came to a head in 403 BCE with an attack by Dionysius of Syracuse, who destroyed the city's walls, enslaved and sold its citizens, and gave its land to the local natives of the area (*Siculi*). This brought about the complete demise of the once proud colony of Naxos.

Wearing his characteristic red shirt, Giuseppe Garibaldi triumphantly leads his troops into Naples. He had spent his last night in the Bay of Naxos, personally repairing his small ship (the *Franklin*), before crossing over to the Calabrian Coast to battle Neapolitan forces at the Volturno River.
Lithograph by F. Ratellier & Co., New York, *c.* 1860 (Wikimedia Commons, PD).

But all was not completely lost. The subsequent amalgamation of the disenfranchised Naxians with their local Siculi neighbors formed a new settlement on the heights of neighboring Mt. Taurus. By the mid-fourth century BCE, other stragglers had been collected from their diaspora and settled beside them on the hill that would eventually become known as Tauromenium, later reduced to Taormina.

Like most of the island, Tauromenium was absorbed into the Roman Province of Sicily during the 240s BCE only to become entangled in a succession of slave revolts (the Servile Wars). These did not end until 71 BCE when the forces of a gladiator-turned-general named Spartacus were crushed at Senerchia n the Italian peninsula. The citadel of Tauromenium, hich had been fortified by rebellious slaves, held ut for a while until—driven by famine—they were etrayed by one of their own, and butchered.

ecognizing the value of its strategic position, Roman mperor Augustus (r. 27 BCE–14 CE) later promoted auromenium to the rank of *colonia*, but not without first eplacing its inhabitants with a new (and loyal) population. Vith this infusion of new blood, the city flourished. Its amous theater, built during the Greek Period and remodeled t least twice by the Romans, is the second largest structure f its type on the island. In his *Historia Naturalis*, Pliny the lder (23–79 CE) makes note of the high esteem in which the ines of the area were held by the people of his day (XIV.8.6).

And Aetna's throat

with roar of frightful
ruin thunders ...

and lifts a cloud of pitch-
black, whirling smoke ...

shooting out globes of flame,
with monster tongues

that lick the stars....

Vergil, *Aeneid*, III:569–579. Adapted

fter the death of Theodosius and the reak-up of the Roman Empire in the ear 395, Sicily became more and more culturally" akin to the Byzantine East han to the Germanic tribes (Vandals and strogoths) that were moving down to ll the vacuum. The ensuing centuries lso witnessed steady Moslem expansion rom the south, culminating in the fall f Taormina (902) and its subsequent ncorporation into the Emirate (Islamic tate) of Sicily *(Imarat Siqilliyya)* with s capital at Palermo. It would be up o Roger Bosso, as the first Norman ount of Sicily, to return the island to he banner of the cross in 1072. There it ould remain for almost eight centuries, erving as a pawn to be traded back and orth among its European neighbors.

his was to change, however, in May of 860 when Giuseppe Garibaldi and his and of "Red Shirts" landed on the island nd defeated the army of the Bourbon ingdom of the Two Sicilies. He established dictatorship that was to last until that ovember when the island was absorbed nto the newly-formed Kingdom of Italy. ess than a century later, at the conclusion

The magnitude of the 1766 eruption of Mount Etna made quite an impact on Sicilian artist Alessandro D'Anna who recorded his impressions with this colored engraving shortly after the event.
Private Collection, Rome (Wikimedia Commons, PD).

of WW II and a long and disastrous Fascist interlude, Sicily was awarded the special status of an autonomous *regione* in the Republic of Italy, and it remains so to this day.

In sum, this area has always been a very special place. In *Italian Journey* (1787), Goethe lauded it as a "paradise on earth," and Gustav Klimt painted a reconstruction of its ancient theater on the ceiling of the Vienna Burgtheater. Taormina became a very popular stop on the itinerary of European elites and *literati* during the 19th and 20th centuries. Nietzsche wrote much of *Thus Spake Zarethusa* there in the 1880s, while D.H. Lawrence admitted that Taormina had filled him with that "good on-the-brink feeling" as he penned *Lady Chatterley's Lover* there in the early 1920s.

The Local Grape Varieties of Etna DOC Wines

The Etna DOC *(Denominazione di Origine Controllata)* consists of a wide band of mineral-rich soils that wrap around the lower slopes of the mountain (between *c*. 400–1200 m above sea level), forming a crescent that is open to the west. This presents growers with a wide range of very challenging microclimates that vary greatly according to the orientation of exposure. Each of these is affected, *inter alia*, by the vagaries of cloud cover, precipitation, and especially by temperatures that exhibit wide diurnal swings. Yet, in spite of these many obstacles, the Etna DOC presents a number of superlative and very distinct wines.

Many consider the Carricante grape to be either the same varietal or a very close relative of Catarratto Bianco, a grape that has also grown on the slopes of Mt. Etna for centuries.
Photo courtesy of Giacomo Ansaldi, *il Consorzio di Tutela Vini DOC Sicilia, Regione Sicilia.*

WHITE GRAPES

The backbone of white wine production in the Etna DOC is the late-ripening **Carricante** (Ker-ih-CAN-tay) grape whose name is derived from the Italian word *carica* (load/loaded) emphasizing the notoriously high yields of this varietal. It challenges growers with a naturally high acidity that requires either a long time on the vine (especially when grown at the higher elevations), or subsequent attention in the winery. Granny Smith apple and citrus predominate on the palate, but this can be rounded through malolactic fermentation, time on the lees, or age in the barrel, taking on hints of honey and even cream. Although a single-varietal Carricante wine is offered by the Baronne di Villagrande Winery and Caselle Cellar Benanti, this grape is usually blended with one of the three less-acetic varieties of the prolific **Catarratto Bianco** (Kah-tar-RAH-to Byan-ko) grape (*Commune, Lucido,* or *Extra Lucido*) that many consider to be the same grape. Also allowed, but less frequently used, is **Minella Bianca** at brings a characteristic hint of anise that is most prominent in Benanti's ıgle varietal (*monovitigno*) **Minella** which they release as an IGP Sicilia wine.

qualify for ETNA BIANCO DOC status a wine must contain a minimum 60% Carricante and, if it contains at least 80% Carricante and that fruit mes from the area around the town of Milo on the eastern face of the lcano, it may be labeled as an ETNA BIANCO SUPERIORE wine.

ED GRAPES

'NA ROSSO DOC wines emphasize three local d grape varietals. The main component is the **erello Mascalese** (Ne-REL-lo Ma-skal-AY-zay) ape, a dark-berried varietal (*nero* = black) that is nsidered to be indigenous to the Mascali Plain the foot of the volcano. Here it still flourishes traditionally head-trained, spur-pruned vines at are supported by chestnut stakes. Although nsitive to the vagaries of individual microclimates, e grape produces fruity (red berry), herbaceous nes with varying degrees of mineral intensity pending on the type of volcanic soil on which it is own. Although single varietal Nerello Mascalese nes are produced by both Benanti and Tenuta rre Nerre, the grape is most commonly utilized in na DOC blends where it must comprise a minimum 80 percent. The remaining fraction is most ten supplied by the related Nerello Cappuccio ape that darkens the ruby color of the Mascalese d twists the flavor profile of the blend more to that of dark, ripe cherries. onovarietal Cappuccio wines are made by both Benanti and by Tenuta di Fessina d are bottled as IGT Sicilia wines. Nerello Mascalese blended with another vorite Sicilian grape, Nero d'Avalo, can also be found, but not in the Etna DOC.

The Nerello Mascalese grape, when blended with its not-too-distant cousin Nerello Cappuccio, perfectly summarizes the terroir of the eastern slopes of the volcano.

Photo courtesy of Giacomo Ansaldi, *il Consorzio di Tutela Vini DOC Sicilia, Regione Sicilia.*

elebrate!

help you celebrate with a perfect bottle of bubbly *(vino spumante)*, one made om grapes hand-picked from the slopes of Europe's most active volcano, Baron nanuele Scammacca del Murgo offers three. All are 100% high-acid Nerello ascalese, all carry the rather nebulous classification of VSQ *(Vino Spumante di ualita)*, and all undergo secondary fermentation in the bottle *(metodo classico)*. **urgo Brut** was the first sparkling wine made from the Mascalese grape and, with fruitier "sister" **Murgo Brut Rosé** (both with 8 g/L of residual sugar) you have o good choices. But don't pass over the **Murgo Extra Brut**. Remuage is done by nd and the lower residual sugar (3 g/L) makes it a much tighter and crisper wine.

Wine Bars & Bottle Shops

In Taormina the *Timoleone Café* at Via Timoleone 6, close to the Teatro Greco, is a great place to take a break if you (or members of your party) cannot decide between a glass of wine, a good craft beer, or an excellent cup of coffee. They are closed in the late afternoon (3:00–6:30 pm). If you want to pick up a bottle to go, stop by *La Torinese*, that has been located conveniently at Corso Umberto 59 since the 1930s. A delight for any gastronome, it carries a wide selection of quality local wines as well as other up-scale products from the area. In Giardini-Naxos, *T. Consiglio*, an *Enoteca* (wine bar) located at Via Naxos 197, offers the area's wines by the glass or bottle (take-away) as well as the local snacks that complement them.

Cannoli dusted with the famous Bronte pistacchia that are grown only on the western slopes of the volcano. It is difficult to eat just one.
Photo courtesy of the Time Traveling Gourmet.

Sweet Tooth

In selecting a sweet (*dolcetto*) from the myriad that are artfully displayed in the shops that you pass, look for something that includes local pistachio nuts. These are not the red-dyed nuts that stained the fingers of our youth, but the *Pistacchia di Bronte*—world famous for the intensity of their color and their flavor. They are grown in and around the village of Bronte on the western slopes of Mt. Etna, a town that was founded by Greek soldiers in the 5th century BCE. A *cannolo* (pl. *cannoli*) with chopped pistachios is always a good bet, freshly assembled for you and served with smiling pride by the person who made it.

Cheers!

In Taormina,
just say

Salute!

(Sah-LOOT-teh)

Valletta

Malta

alletta's Grand Harbor, bulwark of the Knights of Saint John of Jerusalem, and scene of The Great Siege of 1565 that ended forever e Ottoman expansion into the Western Mediterranean.
oto courtesy of the Time Traveling Gourmet.

Valletta, on the Island of Malta, is the main port and capital of the Republic of Malta. Together with the smaller island of Gozo and minuscule Comino, Caminetto, and Filfla they form the Maltese rchipelago, strategically situated about halfway between Europe and Africa, d roughly equidistant between the Strait of Gibraltar and the Suez Canal.

alta derives its name from either the Phoenician word *maleth* ("harbor") or e ancient Greek melite ("honey sweet"), the latter evidently with reference the distinctive honey produced by an indigenous species of honey bee *(Apis ellifera ruttneri)* that evolved there after the islands had become separated om the mainland of Europe. The Romans simply Latinized the name to *elita*, as it was known when the Apostle Paul was shipwrecked there (Acts viii.1), and the name was passed on to succeeding centuries as Malta.

Grand Master António Manoel de Vilhena kneels before St. Jean who presents him with the banner of the Order of Malta on a gold *zecchino* (sequin), minted in 1725.
Photo courtesy of the Classical Numismatic Group LLC, CNG 87, Lot 1876.

spite of a human history that stretches back well into the Stone Age, and e fact that Malta has been the site of two of the most crucial battles in all of ıropean history, it is ironic that the island derives much of its modern fame from a small bird: a sub-species of the Peregrine Falcon. And it is not a living and breathing *Falco peregrinos brookei* at that, but a jewel-encrusted statuette that formed the centerpiece of a 1940s detective novel. Its plot recalled, somewhat incorrectly, the annual rent that was paid to Charles V by the Knights of Saint John of Jerusalem for their use of the Maltese Archipelago. Charles' foresight in allowing the Knights to settle on, and fortify, Malta proved to be most fortuitous for they transformed the island into a bulwark on Europe's southern flank. In September of 1565, after what was to become known as The Great Siege, the Knights defeated the much larger forces of Suleiman the Magnificent, and ended forever the Ottoman aspirations of expansion into the Western Mediterranean.

A photo of the movie prop that artist Fred Sexton made for John Huston for use in *The Maltese Falcon* (Warner Brothers, 1941).
Photograph used with the permission of Hank Risan (PD).

Following this victory, the 67 year-old Grand Master of the Knights, Jean Parisot de la Valette, began to build a new, fortified city across the harbor from the Knights' stronghold of Fort St. Angelo. When completed, the city would be given his name and would remain the home of the Knights of St. John for centuries.

Over the years the Knights attracted an eclectic membership to the island. In 1607 a young Italian artist named Michelangelo Merisi da Caravaggio sought refuge with them after killing a man in a bar fight in Rome. Once accepted into the Order, Caravaggio set to work painting a huge (12 × 17 feet) canvas that depicted the beheading of Saint John, the patron saint of the Order. This painting, now beautifully displayed in Valletta (Oratory of St. John's Co-Cathedral), is the only one of Caravaggio's masterpieces that bears his signature—hidden in the dripping blood of the saint. The artist continued to be a brawler, however, and after seriously wounding a fellow Knight, he was proclaimed to be "a foul and rotten member" and expelled from the Order.

Jean Parisot de la Valette (1554–1642), the 49th Grand Master of the Knights of St. John of Jerusalem, and the hero of The Great Siege of 1565.
A copper engraving by Laurent Cars, *c.* 1725 (Wikimedia Commons, PD).

The Knights retained their island stronghold until 1798 when they were forced to leave by Napoleon whose harsh treatment of the Maltese people drove them to seek protection from Great Britain. Subsequently in 1814, as part of the Treaty of Paris, Malta officially became a British Crown Colony. Relative peace, coupled with the island's healthy climate soon began to attract a host of Victorian notables and ne'er-do-wells. Lord Byron visited the island often, and Benjamin Disraeli considered Valletta to be one of the "most beautiful of cities," while the fortitude and tenacity displayed by the Knights during The Great Siege would continue to fascinate Sir Walter Scott until his death in 1832.

Courage has always been the hallmark of the people of Malta. In World War II, during the Second Great Siege, more than 7000 tons of Axis explosives were dropped on "Fortress Malta" in just six weeks, earning it the unenviable title of the most intensely bombed place on earth. For their bravery, in 1942, the people of Malta were awarded the George Cross as a witness to their "heroism and devotion that will long be famous in history."

1974, the Republic of Malta finally became a free and independent
ation and, in May of 2004, it joined the European Union.

ocal Grape Varietals

Michelangelo Merisi da Caravaggio, a chalk portrait by Ottavio Leoni, *c.* 1621.
Biblioteca Marucelliana, Florence (Wikimedia Commons, PD).

ecause the Maltese Archipelago has served as a stepping-stone r so many cultures throughout the centuries, it is impossible determine which group arrived on the island with the wine ape *(vitis vinifera)* in its baggage. The Phoenicians—sometime the 8th century BCE—are usually given the credit. Today is estimated that as many as one hundred different wine ape varietals are grown in the archipelago, including many pular international varietals such as Chardonnay, Shiraz, and bernet Sauvignon. Two grapes, however, the red Gellewza and e white Girgentina boast Maltese pedigrees. They may have en brought by those early Phoenicians who also left traces of eir Semitic language that still survive to the present day.

hen Malta joined the European Union, government support for the local ne industry was removed. Winemakers who had been more or less self-gulating were forced to compete directly with wines made in other EU untries that were often better and cheaper. In order to enhance the quality their wines, and to make them more competitive, Maltese winemakers, gether with the government, put into effect a set of strict protocols. ese are similar to the appellation systems used elsewhere in the EU.

is combination of regulation and competition has caused tremendous vancements to be made in Maltese wines that are exemplified the offerings of the two early pillars of the Maltese wine dustry: Delicata, founded by Emmanuel Delicata in 1907, and arsovin, begun by Anthony Cassar in 1919. Both of these pioneer mpanies emphasize wines that include indigenous or traditional altese grapes. Meridiana, on the other hand, founded in the 80s by Mark Farrugia (now in technological partnership with ntinori) produces a slate of wines that emphasize international rietals grown in the archipelago. These wines are bottled under mes that celebrate Malta's rich Phoenician heritage such as **is** (100% Chardonnay), honoring a goddess popular in Phoenicia well as Egypt, and **Bel** (100% Shiraz), named for another mitic deity who appears often in the Biblical text as Ba'al.

Girgentina, Malta's traditional white grape.
Photograph courtesy of Georges Meekers.

HITE GRAPES

e white **Girgentina** (Gir-gen-TEEN-a) grape may derive name from the ancient Greek town of Girgento/Agrigento Southwestern Sicily, an hypothesis that is strengthened by

Gellewza, Malta's traditional red grape.
Photograph courtesy of Georges Meekers.

the grape's physical similarity to the Inzolia/Isolia grape that is grown extensively in that area today. Marsovin's **La Torre Girgentina** (I.G.T.), made from 100% Girgentina, illustrates the grape's complexity, displaying crisp (green) apple flavors that fade to ripe melon over a mineral base. The grape also blends well with international varietals producing fresh, full-flavored wines such as Delicata's **Medina** blend of Girgentina and Chardonnay.

RED GRAPES

Gellewza (Jel-LOZ-a) appears to derive its name from the Arabic *geloz* ("nut") or a similar Persian word meaning "hazelnut" or "walnut," apparently with reference to the size and shape of the berries. Delicata's **Maltese Falcon Rosé** (I.G.T.), made from 100% Gellewza is a very approachable, medium-dry wine with great color and powerful strawberry and red fruit flavors throughout. The grape is also used quite successfully in crafting semi-sparkli wines (see below). It blends well with Shiraz to produce soft, but firm, food-friendly red wines, as well as fruity, often tart, rosés.

It is said that during the tourist season there are at least three thirsty tourists on th islands for every Maltese resident and, at present, there is simply not enough land under grape cultivation to provide winemakers with the fruit to meet that demand. Accordingly, some wineries regularly import freshly picked grapes from Italy, shipping them in refrigerated containers to Malta. Here they are processed after th earlier-ripening, locally grown grapes have been pressed. With the 2009 vintage a system was put in place in which an individually numbered paper strip (a *banderol* is placed around the neck of each bottle. These provide instant recognition that the wine is made from grapes grown in the Maltese Archipelago as well as citing the appellation (DOK or IGT) for which that particular wine has qualified.

A Special Treat

In 2011, Marsovin released **Primus**, a sweet wine made from the local Gellewza grape blended with Shiraz. This was the first Maltese wine to be awarded the D.O.K. classification *"Imqadded Ta' Malta."* It presents rich flavors of dried fruit and cherr with a long and pleasant finish. Marsovin also makes a 100% Shiraz *passito* named **Guze** (Joo-SE), the nickname of Joseph Cassar, one of the company's early pioneers.

Celebrate!

On Malta, everyday can be a celebration, with readily available and very affordable semi-sparkling *(frizzante)* wines made from the indigenous varietals. Crisp and clean, Delicata's **Girgentina Frizzante Brut Blanc de Blanc** (Lifestyle Series) is a delight. Slightly sweeter are Delicata's **Gellewza Frizzante Rosé Demi Sec**

Wine Words To Watch For

The following designations are readily encountered on Maltese wine labels.

- **D.O.K.** *(Denominazzjoni ta' Origini Kontrollata)* indicates that the wine has been crafted exclusively from specific varietals grown by registered farmers on either Malta (D.O.K. Malta) or Gozo (D.O.K. Gozo) according to specified maximum yields, and has been vinified according to clearly stated standards. Each wine is then sent to a laboratory for organoleptic analysis by a professional wine tasting panel.

- **I.G.T.** *(Indikazzjoni Geografika Tipika)* usually appears on the label as I.G.T. Maltese Islands and certifies that, although the wine may be a blend of grapes from vineyards on Malta and Gozo, it has been produced according to specific, although less stringent, production protocols than those required for D.O.K. status. It does not require an organoleptic analysis, although random samples are analyzed regularly in order to maintain quality.

- **Imqaddad** (pronounced "im-ADD-ed" without the "Q") refers to the Maltese practice of sun-drying seasonal produce for use later in the year (*imqaddad tadám* are sun-dried tomatoes). Here, the term is reserved exclusively for a wine in which 100% of the grapes have been naturally dried in the sun (not cold-dried) after harvest. The drying of the grapes builds the sugars, increases the potential alcohol level, and concentrates the flavors. Known elsewhere as *passito*, the technique goes back at least to the time of the Phoenicians.

- **Superior** on a Maltese wine label does not necessarily indicate a wine of superior or higher quality but rather a wine whose percentage of alcohol is slightly higher than the minimum alcohol requirement for a quality wine with that particular appellation (DOK or IGT).

ifestyle Series) and Marsovin's **Gellewza Rosé** (Sottovoce Series) both of which splay an abundance of sliced strawberry on the nose as well on as the palate.

ıt if only a true *méthode traditionnelle* sparkler will suffice for your special event, arsovin makes a very tasty one from Chardonnay grapes grown on its Wardija ılley Estate. Named **Cassar de Malte** after the company's founder, a bottle can difficult to find since it has a very limited annual production (*c.* 500 cases).

Georges Meekers, author of *Wines of Malta – The Essential Guide* and founder of Wine Campus.

Photo courtesy of the Time Traveling Gourmet.

Bite To Eat

you appreciate the wines made from traditional Maltese grapes, consider iring them with traditional Maltese cuisine at *Nenu the Artisan Baker* 43 St. Domenic Street). There, master baker and owner, Nenu Debono has tegrated a multi-media celebration of Malta's culinary past with a spotless, odern restaurant featuring an antique stone oven. Try *Ftira* (FTIR-ah), a crusty ead base (from a closely guarded recipe) embellished with a wide range of ppings: like a pizza, only better! Finish with one of Zeppi's local liquors made om prickly pear, fennel, or the honey produced by that indigenous honeybee.

you dine, life-size manikins will demonstrate the steps of baking in the ditional Maltese manner while several television screens document the odern method of creating the perfect Ftira (complete with English sub-titles).

Life-size manikins demonstrate traditional Maltese baking methods at Nenu the Artisan Baker on St. Domenic Street.
Photo courtesy of the Time Traveling Gourmet.

Bottle Shops

The Wembley Store (established in 1924) at 305 Republic Street is a specialty food shop conveniently located just inside Valletta's City Gate. They offer a wide selection of cheeses, charcuterie, and othe fine foods on the ground floor, but don't miss their wine cellar (the stairs are on the right as you enter). Their huge inventory and knowledgeable staff combine to make for easy, one-stop shopping

Beer

When thirst calls for a beer, try Cisk or Cisk Export. Both are bottom-fermented lagers and will quench your thirst without robbing you of the rest of your day. Brewed in the archipelago since 1928 (and now part of Farsons Group), Cisk also makes Excel, a low-carbohydrate brew and a Cisk Extra Strong (9 %) known locally as XS. Cisk Chill, a light, lemon-flavored lager with a relatively low alcohol level (4 %) is great in the heat of the summer. Farsons also makes Blue Label, a British Mild Ale, and Hopleaf, a traditional English Pale Ale.

A great place to enjoy that brew is at *The Pub,* located just around the corner from the Grand Master's Palace at 136 Archbishop Street. It is known locally as Ollie's Last Pub in memory of actor Oliver Reed, star of such films as *Women in Love* and *Oliver*. He passed away after spending a notorious afternoon there in May of 1999, when he was engaged in filming *Gladiator,* in which he played the part of Proximo, Russell Crowe's mentor.

The Pub (aka *Ollie's Last Pub*) on Archbishop Street has become a memorial to actor Oliver Reed who died in Valletta while filming *Gladiator.*
Photo courtesy of the Time Traveling Gourmet.

Cheers!

In Valletta,
just say

Sahha!

(SAH-hah)

Thank You.
The author has benefited greatly from conversations with Georges Meekers, the author of *Wines of Malta – The Essential Guide,* wine correspondent for *Times of Malta,* and founder of Wine Campus, an international, on-line wine school (www.winecampus.net).

Venice

taly

e Basilica of St Mark *(Basilica di San Marco)* from the Grand Canal. Founded as a small trading post in the Adriatic marshes in 421, nice would one day overcome its humble roots to become the dominant military and commercial power in the Mediterranean.
oto courtesy of the Time Traveling Gourmet.

Unlike most Italian ports, Venice *(Venezia)* cannot boast a lengthy Roman pedigree. While emperors spread their rule across the Mediterranean, the area that would later become Venice remained a literal backwater, pulated mainly by fishermen and fugitives. The minds of those who sought the elter and seclusion of the offshore islands offered fertile ground for nascent ristianity. And so Saint Peter dispatched the Evangelist Mark to preach nong them. In this task, Mark was so successful that he was promoted to the nk of Bishop and sent on to Egypt where he continued his apostolic labors Alexandria. But, before he left the shores of the lagoon, an angel appeared Mark with the promise that one day he would be buried in Venice.

Doge Andrea Dandolo (*c.* 1344–1382) kneels before the figure of St. Mark on a Venetian gold *zecchino.*
Museo Correr, Venice. Photo by Sailko (Wikimedia Commons, CC BY 3.0).

as, the angel's prophesy of a Venetian burial was to be delayed. Mark grew old d, after suffering martyrdom in the year 68, was buried beneath the church at he had founded in Alexandria. There he would remain until 828 when Doge ustiniano Participazio commissioned two Venetian merchants to steal his

The Lion of St. Mark, symbol of the Serene Republic of Venice. Tempera on canvas by Vittore Carpaccio (*c.* 1516).
The Doge's Palace Collection, Venice (Google Arts Project, PD).

body and bring it back to Venice. This task was accomplished by packing the saint's remains in a shipment of pork and spiriting them out of Egypt, literally under the noses of cringing Moslem inspectors. The angel's promise had been fulfilled. The relics of the saint became the spiritual cornerstone of the basilica that bears his name. Mark—portrayed as a winged lion—would become the patron saint and intellectual cornerstone of the Most Serene Republic of Venice—*La Serenissima*—that would one day rule the Mediterranean World.

"Pax tibi Marce, evangelista meus. Hic requiescat corpus tuum."

May Peace be with you, Mark, my Evangelist. Here your body will lie in rest.

Precariously situated between the Holy Roman Empire to the west and the Byzantine Empire to the east, Venice rose to power through a long succession of capable leaders *(Doges)* and their cunning diplomatic strategies. By the time that Pope Innocent III called for the Fourth Crusade to liberate the Holy Land in 1202, an elderly, blind Doge named Enrico Dandolo had inserted himself—and Venice—squarely into the enterprise. He had offered to provide the ships and sailors to transport the knights and their equipment. Even when the Crusade was diverted in order to attack Constantinople, Doge Dandolo was there: leading the charge, dividing the spoils, and sending the best of the loot home to Venice.

Perhaps the most visible reminder of the extent of the Crusaders' looting are four gilt-bronze horses, copies of which now adorn the *loggia* on the West Façade of St. Mark's Basilica. These had originally been brought to Constantinople as booty by Constantine the Great in the 4th century. For the next 600 years they would keep the igil, observing with masked emotion as the shifting history of Venice nfolded at their feet. This was a story punctuated time after me by the return of the plague known as the Black Death.

1797, however, the horses lost their role as observant ystanders and became full participants. Forced by apoleon Bonaparte's victorious army, the Great ouncil of Venice assembled and immediately voted self out of existence. French forces filled the Piazza nd the four were dragged off to Paris where they ould be placed, as symbols of triumph and victory, top the *Arc de Triomphe du Carrousel.* Sadly, they ere but a small portion of what many describe as apoleon's "rape" of the art treasures of Europe.

The wily Enrico Dandolo, 41st Doge of Venice, who supervised the siege and looting of Constantinople, was buried in that city in 1205.

Engraving by an unknown artist. 19th century, Italian (Wikimedia Commons, PD).

ortunately, their Parisian exile was relatively brief, thanks the intervention of the famous Neoclassical sculptor ntonio Canova. Born in Asolo, at the foot of the Venetian lps, Canova had been summoned to Paris in 1802 to model bust of the emperor. While there, he worked tirelessly retrieve many of the art treasures that Napoleon had tolen—including the horses of St. Mark's Basilica.

ack on the loggia, the foursome resumed its vigil in 1815, the year that the Congress f Vienna placed the city under Habsburg rule as part of the new Kingdom of ombardy-Venetia. Talk in the cafés below them slowly changed from the frivolous anter of the decadent ays to more revolutionary lk of unification with ther states on the alian Peninsula. Such leas became more ommon in 1846 after e Lagoon was bridged y the Milan–Venice ailway. But the coal- urning, smoke-belching ngines also brought ith them the pollution at would later present e greater problem.

The West Façade of the Basilica di San Marco from the piazza below. The famous horses are in the loggia above the central portal.

Photo by Ricardo André Frantz (Wikimedia Commons, PD).

he 20th century opened ith the collapse of St. lark's famous *Campanile.*

The Bronze Horses of the Basilica di San Marco were brought to Venice after the army of the Fourth Crusade sacked Constantinople in 1204.
Photo by Gianfranco Zanovello (Wikimedia Commons, CC BY-SA 4.0).

The ruins of St. Mark's *Campanile* after its collapse on July 14, 1902.
Unknown photographer. Shchusev State Museum of Architecture (Wikimedia Commons, PD).

Having guided ships to port and palace for almost a millennium, the tower crashed into the piazza in 1902, covering it with a thick blanket of brick dust. While the tower was rebuilt over the next decade, the storm clouds of WWI began to gather. Accordingly, the horses were trotted south to the safety of Rome, while the youth of the Veneto was sent northward to train and to die on the banks of the Isonzo and Piave Rivers.

The armistice offered little peace for Italy, as Benito Mussolini and his black-shirted Fascists came to power. In 1934, *Il Duce* traveled to Venice to welcome his future ally Adolf Hitler on his first official visit outside of Germany. After the two megalomaniacs led their respective countries—and Europe—into complete disaster, Europe worked itself back to become the industrial giant that it is today. But, with this rebirth, the curse of air pollution returned as well. By the early 1980s, the threat of damage to the horses had caused them to be taken down and placed inside the basilica, while their place on the loggia was taken by replicas. Let us hope that their tenure will be more peaceful.

Prosecco

While the Veneto is home to many great wines, the one most readily associated with Venice is Prosecco (Pro-SEK-ko), a low-alcohol, sparkling wine whose roots disappear into our most remote past. Some would trace them back to *vinum Pucinum,* a wine from the area that was discussed by Pliny the Elder who died in the eruption of Mt. Vesuvius in 79. The Roman elites of the time stressed its health-giving properties and Livia, the third wife of Emperor Augustus, is said to have consumed *Pucinum* exclusively until the day she died—at the grand age of 86!

ıe Entity Formerly Known as Prosecco

The traditional Prosecco grape now known as Glera forms the backbone of Venice's sparkling wines.
Photo courtesy of Masottina, Conegliano. Italy.

aditionally, the word "Prosecco" has referred t only to a specific grape varietal, but also to the ce where that grape was grown (throughout e area of Conegliano and Valdobbiadene in the ovince of Treviso), as well as the type of wine ually sparkling) that the grape produced. wever, things were to change in 2009.

osecco as Place

a place name, the spelling variant *Proseccho,* pears in the 14th century in reference to a lage that is now a suburb of Trieste. It seems be related to the word *prosek* meaning "a path ough the woods." Fynes Moryson, a British veler in the 1590s, appears to have been the first refer to the wine from that area as Prosecco.

osecco as Grape

2009, in an effort to protect the homeland m "Prosecco" produced in Australia and ewhere, the name of the Prosecco grape s changed. It was reincarnated as one its less frequently encountered synonyms: **Glera** (GLEH-rah).

osecco as Wine

osecco must consist of a minimum of 85% Glera and, while many ıes are 100% Glera, the juice of one or more of the following native pes—often the result of field blends—may be present:

erdiso (Ver-DEE-zo) – a grape that was saved from extinction by Giuseppe occhetti in the 1960s. It is now grown mostly in the Treviso Hills between onegliano (Con-eg-LYA-no) and Valdobbiadene (Val-do-BYA-di-ne).

ianchetta (Byan-KHET-ta) – a grape with a tendency toward stringency. Small quantities have been grown for centuries in and round Treviso (hence the variant Bianchetta Trevigiana).

erera (Pe-REH-ra) – a disease-sensitive varietal that derives its name either from s pear-shaped clusters of fruit or the flavor that it is said to impart to the base ine. It has been traditionally grown in the neighborhood of Valdobbiadene.

like Champagne, which undergoes its secondary (bubble-producing) mentation in the bottle (*méthode champenoise* or Classic Method), the

Italian Wine Classifications in descending order

DOCG	*Denominazione di Origine Controllata e Garantita*	Controlled and Guaranteed Designation of Origin
DOC DOP	*Denominazione di Origine Controllata* *Denominazione di Origine Protetta*	Controlled Designation of Origin Protected Designation of Origin
IGT	*Indicazione Geographica Tipica*	Typical of a Geographic Indication/Designation

secondary fermentation of Prosecco takes place in a large metal tank called an autoclave, and is subsequently bottled under pressure. This method *(Metodo Charmat-Martinotti)*, invented by Federico Martinotti in 1895 and adapted by Eugène Charmat in 1907, was to revolutionize the wine industry in the Veneto.

Prosecco/Glera wine may appear in three styles:

Vineyards in the Treviso Hills near Valdobbiadene.
Photo by Luca Temporelli (Wikimedia Commons, CC BY-SA 2.0).

- *Prosecco Tranquillo,* a still wine that is difficult to find because most customers expect a wine with bubbles,
- *Prosecco Frizzante,* a lightly or semi-sparkling wine that has undergone only a partial secondary fermentation resulting in a fairly low pressure (2.5 bars) inside the bottle.
- *Prosecco Spumante,* a foamy or fully sparkling wine that has undergone a nearly complete secondary fermentation resulting in a higher pressure (3.6 bars) inside the bottle.

Prosecco is authorized in three degrees of sweetness according to French/EU regulations, based on the number of grams of residual sugar per liter (g/l). They are Brut (less than 12 g/l), Extra Dry (between 12–17 g/l), and Dry (between 17–32 g/l).

Since the changes of 2009, the word Prosecco has become a geographical denominator for wines made from Glera grapes that are grown in the area of Conegliano and Valdobbiadene (about 30 iles NE of Venice the Province Treviso) and solo (Ah-SO-lo), ong the *Colli solani* ridge at e foot of the enetian Alps. At e same time, these ines were awarded

A paper strip (*fascetta*) at the neck of the bottle calls attention to the wine's DOC or DOCG status of quality.
Photo: Conegliano Valdobbiadene DOCG.

OCG status and the spumante version was allowed to be labeled with the rase *Prosecco Superiore.* In addition, the neck of each bottle must bear a special aper strip (*fascetta*) bearing "DOCG" and a unique identifying number.

hen dealing with *Prosecco Superiore* there are two additional words to watch for. ne term *Rive* calls attention to the specific terroir of a particular village or hamlet *razione)* of the DOCG area and must appear on the label along with the vintage ear. *Cartizze* refers to the flagship subzone of the territory (*c.* 250 steep acres SW Valdobbiadine) and will also appear on the label or paper strip. Most Cartizze ines are bottled Dry or Extra Dry and are thus a little sweeter. Expect to pay a remium of two to three times the regular price, but these wines are well worth it!

ne IGT wines previously produced in that area now carry DOC status and may be beled "Prosecco" (but not *Superiore*). Each bottle will bear a *fascetta* identifying it a DOC wine.

lthough we do not know how either Pucinum or the earliest Prosecco was ade, or how it tasted, we might get a hint from a type of wine that was roduced in the area before the appearance of the autoclave in the 1970s. After rimary fermentation in open tanks, these wines were allowed to ferment second time on their lees, in the bottle. This produced wines that could e described as clear (*limpido*), cloudy (*torpido*), or anywhere in between. ften these DOCG wines have been stored vertically after bottling and are ecanted before they are served. Azienda Agricola Ca' dei Zago, founded 1924, produces similar frizzante wines from Glera grapes grown on six ectares in Valdobbiadene (with small additions of Verdiso, Bianchetta, and erera). In addition to exhibiting a bright, citrusy character, these wines are ften described as being "salty"—and some would even say "crunchy."

ost Prosecco/Glera is consumed young: when it is fresh, fragrant, and aunting its fruity (golden apple, peach, and pear) and floral (lilac and acacia) harms. But never pass up the chance to taste a Prosecco with a little age. And, njoy it as the Venetians do, from a large tulip-shaped glass rather than the ute or *coupe* associated with the more complex wines of Champagne.

Entrance to one of the many *Bacari* in Venice. *Bacaro* is the ancient local name for a bar/restaurant that offers a quick bite and a glass of wine.
Photo by mickamroch (Wikimedia Commons, CC BY 2.0).

Wine Bars & Bottle Shops

Bistrot de Venise (Calle dei Fabri, San Marco) is the place to visit for those interested in Venetian wine and food and how both reflect and define the local culture. A great selection of wines by the glass is available at the bar, poured and discussed by a very knowledgeable staff. This combination of a good selection and a knowledgeable staff is shared by these bottle shops: *Vino E .... Vini* – "inland" from the Ponte del Sepulcro near the Hotel La Residenza; *Millevini Enoteca* – between the Rialto Bridge and the Campo San Bartolomeo; and *Non Solo Vino* between the Campo S. Maurizio and the Fondamenta de la Malvasia Vecchia.

Thank You.

The author wishes to thank Alan Tardi of the *Consorzio Tutela del Vino Conegliano Valdobbiadene Prosecco* for his very helpful conversations about Prosecco and the wines of the Veneto.

Cheers!

In Venice,
just say

Cin Cin!

(chin-chin)

ndex

Additional Photo Credits

The main attribution for each illustration accompanies it in the text. Supplemental information for Wikimedia Commons files by page is offered here. Http://commons.wikimedia.org/wiki/File:

(1) Tetradrachm_Athens_480-420BC_MBA_Lyon.jpg
(2) Bust Athena Velletri Glyptothek Munich 213.jpg
(2) Veduta del Castello d'Acropolis dalla parte di Tramontana - Fanelli Francesco - 1695.jpg
(5) Retsina.jpg
(7) Μνημείο του Λυσικράτη 6122.jpg
(9) Nativity Facade of Sagrada Família - 2013.07 - panoramio.jpg
(10) Mosaic de les Tres Gràcies.jpg
(13) Ramon Casas - 4 Gats - Google Art Project.jpg
(15) Modello Cavallo di Troia.jpg
(15) Stater Lampsacus 360-340BC obverse CdM Paris.jpg
(16) Briseis Phoinix Louvre G152.jpg
(17) Evelyn de Morgan - Hero Holding the Beacon for Leander, 1885.jpg
(18) Grapes of İzmir.jpg
(18) Amphorae stacking.jpg
(19) Banquet Assos Louvre Ma2829.jpg
(19) Laocoon Pio-Clementino Inv1059-1064-1067.jpg
(21) Forte Michelangelo 2018 Blick vom Hafen.jpg
(22) Exekias Dionysos Staatliche Antikensammlungen 2044.jpg
(24) Ugni blanc raisin.jpg
(25) Montalcino 002.jpg
(26) Tarquinia Tomb of the Leopards.jpg
(26) Capitoline she-wolf Musei Capitolini MC1181.jpg
(27) Dubrovnik as seen from Srđ - September 2017.jpg
(29) Orlando Sculpture.jpg
(29) Main street-Dubrovnik-2.jpg
(30) Saracen fleet against Crete.jpg
(31) Marco Polo - costume tartare.jpg
(32) Onofrio's Fountain, Dubrovnik, Croatia.jpg
(33) Venitian Fortress of Koules.jpg
(33) 001-knossos-01.jpg
(34) Pasiphae Minotauros Cdm Paris DeRidder1066 detail.jpg
(34) Dionysus, marble bust Knossos, 2nd century AD, AMH, 145410.jpg
(35) Vathypetro 1.jpg
(39) Hagia Sophia Mars 2013.jpg
(39) Coinage with Byzas 2nd 3rd century CE.jpg
(40) Venezia Basilica di San Marco Innen Quadriga 2.jpg
(40) Mustafa Kemal Pasha Time magazine Vol. I No. 4 Mar. 24, 1923.jpg
(41) Benjamin-Constant-The Entry of Mahomet II into Constantinople-1876.jpg
(44) Hagia Sophia Southwestern entrance mosaics 2.jpg
(45) Limassol Hafen UN.jpg
(47) Kolossi Castle 01.jpg
(47) Caterina Cornaro by Gentile Bellini.jpg
(50) Maratheftiko, cépage noir de Chypre.jpg
(52) Mosaics in the House of Dionysus (I) (5030266269).jpg; Mosaics in the House of Dionysus (III) (5030268893).jpg
(53) Port of Málaga, Northeast view 20090412 1.jpg

(54) Liberación de los cautivos de Málaga por los Reyes Católicos (Museo de Málaga).jpg
(55) Picasso monument Malaga.jpg
(56) Weißer Elbling Traube03b.jpg
(59) Tétradrachme de la cité de Rhodes à l'effigie d'Hélios.jpg
(60) Colossus of Rhodes.jpg
(64) Embonas 851 08, Greece - panoramio (1).jpg
(67) Temenos des Artemidoros (Alt-Thera) 02.jpg
(73) Taormina-Teatro Greco01.jpg
(73, 74) Drachma, Naxos, Sicily, 530-510 BC.jpg
(74) Garibaldi-Entrée à Naples - lith. of Ratellier & Co., New York. LCCN00650825.jpg
(75) Eruzione dell'Etna del 1766, incisione colorata di Alessandro D'Anna.jpg
(80) Maltese Falcon film prop created by Fred Sexton for John Huston.jpg
(80) Jean La Valette.jpg
(81) Bild-Ottavio Leoni, Caravaggio.jpg
(85) Andrea dandolo, zecchino, 1343-1354.jpg
(86) Leone marciano andante - Vittore Carpaccio - Google Cultural Institute.jpg
(87) EnricoDandolo.jpg
(87) Veneza47.jpg
(88) "Dolce sguardo bronzeo".jpg
(88) Ruins of St Mark's Campanile.jpg
(90) ProseccoSanVito.jpg
(92) 07 - ITALY - Bacaro (osteria) Veneziano - Venetian Gourmet restaurant high quality.jpg

Notes